# MEDIEVAL IRISH LYRICS

SELECTED & TRANSLATED

*by*

JAMES CARNEY

UNIVERSITY OF CALIFORNIA PRESS

BERKELEY AND LOS ANGELES : 1967

*For the memory of my father*
*PATRICK CARNEY*
*from Kiltimagh*
*and of my mother*
*CONSTANCE GRACE*
*from Thomastown*

---

*University of California Press*
*Berkeley and Los Angeles, California*

*Library of Congress Catalog Card Number 67-16657*

*Printed in the Republic of Ireland at the Dolmen Press Ltd.*

# CONTENTS

# INTRODUCTION

The title of the present work 'Medieval Irish Lyrics' calls for some explanation, if not indeed for apology. Certain possible titles—all of which would have been open to some objection—had been pre-empted: 'Ancient Irish Poetry' by Kuno Meyer, 'Early Irish Lyrics' by Gerard Murphy, and 'Early Irish Poetry' by myself. There remained to me the possibility of calling the present work 'Medieval Irish Lyrics' with the unhappy consciousness that the term 'medieval' was being somewhat misapplied to certain poems in the collection. The first difficulty, of course, is that the book contains Gaelic poems and poems in Latin written by Irishmen. Every language in using such terms as 'old,' 'medieval' and 'modern' has its own internal categorization. In Latin we may correctly regard any poem written, say about 600 A.D., as 'medieval.' But a poem written in Gaelic at that date, or indeed three centuries subsequently, would be classed as 'old.' We may end this apology with a word of direction to the reader. All the Latin poems printed here are correctly labelled 'medieval,' having regard to the internal categorization of Latin. The Gaelic poems which have been dated in the notes from the seventh to the tenth century are, in the internal categorization of Irish, 'old' rather than 'medieval.' Linguistically the medieval period in Irish ends about 1250 A.D., so there are four poems which could be classed as 'early modern' (XXXVII, XLI) or 'modern' (VIII, XL). But for these I feel that less apology is needed. The division of the Irish language into 'old' (600-900 A.D.), 'medieval' (900-1250 A.D.), 'early modern' (1250-1700 A.D.) and 'modern' (1700, onwards) is a purely linguistic classification. The Gaelic language in Ireland remained comparatively untouched by the two great events that ushered in the modern world, the Renaissance and the Reformation. Consequently, from a general European point of view much of the folk material recorded in Ireland in recent decades may properly be regarded as reflecting the medieval rather than the modern world, being medieval in spirit if not in language. Indeed, so traditional are contemporary Irish folk tales that they cling to the notion of a world of three continents so that if one sails far enough into the western ocean one will come, not to America, but to walls of brass which are in fact the horizon.

## IRISH METRES

A very few years ago any scholar writing on Irish metres would begin with the statement that the verse forms generally used in Irish in the period 600-900 A.D. derive from an early Irish imitation of the verse forms of Latin hymns. The similarities are that in Irish verse and in Latin hymns there is a division into quatrains, the lines are based upon a syllable count, usually consisting of seven or eight syllables, and use is made of rhyme. The following quatrain may be quoted as an example of the metre of a Latin hymn; it is from a poem to the Virgin Mary, written in the eighth century by an Irish monk called Cú Cuimne:

> Cantemus in omni die
> concinentes varie
> conclamantes Deo dignum
> ymnum sanctae Marie

The metre of this poem is virtually identical with an Irish metre called *sétna mór*. The syllable pattern is $8^2 + 7^3 + 8^2 + 7^3$, using the formula with which it is usual to describe Irish metres;[1] *varie* rhymes with *Marie*, and, whether intentional or not, there is *deibide* rhyme (about which we will speak below) between *die* and *varie*; there is internal rhyme between *dignum* and *ymnum*. In this verse, of course, the similarities between Latin hymn metres and Irish verse forms are exaggerated. The Irish monk is introducing specific Irish features into the Latin metre known as trochaic tetrameter catalectic of which a pre-Christian example is found in the marching song of Caesar's soldiers:

> Gallias Caesar subègit
> Nicomedes Caesarem.
> Ecce Caesar nunc triùmphat
> qui subegit Gallias.

The syllabic pattern is here also $8^2 + 7^3 + 8^2 + 7^3$, but the typical Irish features of rhyme and internal rhyme are absent.[2]

But the dependence of Irish metres upon Latin hymns has been gravely exaggerated. A brilliant article published in 1963 by Professor Calvert Watkins of Harvard has demonstrated quite clearly that Irish syllabic verse in many of its features is derived from primitive Irish verse forms; he reaches the very important conclusion that 'We

---

1. The large numbers tell the number of syllables in each of the four lines. The superior numbers tell the number of syllables in the last word of the line.
2. In the final words the rhythmical pattern is, of course, counted from the accent (*subègit, triùmphat*).

can now add Irish to the list of languages, Greek, Vedic, and Slavic, which have preserved the metrical form of Indo-European poetry.'[3]

Irish metrics is a wide and complicated subject. Here we can hope to do no more than to make a few comments which will, it is hoped, give the reader some appreciation of the technicalities of the Irish verse-forms in the present volume.[4]

Rhyme became an essential part of Irish verse, but it is not part of its ancient Indo-European inheritance. The following archaic poem, which is in a metre of obscure structure, and not apparently syllabic, shows an early tentative experiment with rhyme:

> Ind ráith i comair in dairfedo,
> ba Bruidgi, ba Cathail,
> ba Aedo, ba Ailello,
> ba Conaing, ba Cuilíni,
> ocus ba Máele Dúin.
> Ind ráith d'éis cach ríg ar úair,
> ocus int slúaig, foait i n-úir.[5]

---

3. *Celtica* VI, 249.
4. The reader is referred to Gerard Murphy, *Early Irish Metrics*, Dublin, 1961; Eleanor Knott on Irish Classical Poetry (In *Early Irish Literature*, Eleanor Knott, Gerard Murphy, Introduction by James Carney, Routledge and Kegan Paul, London, 1965, pp. 21-92). These works are to be read in the light of the article by Professor Watkins referred to above.
5. The rhyme is, of course, between *Dúin* and *úir*. The text of the poem is substantially as given by Murphy, *Early Irish Lyrics*, p. xvi.

'The fort beside the oak-grove
was Bruidge's, was Cathal's,
was Conaing's, was Cuilíne's
and it was Máel Dúin's.
One by one, the kings sleep in the earth
and the fort still endures.'

Speaking of the beginnings of rhyme, we may quote the
words of Professor Francis Byrne: 'The origins of rhyme
are very obscure: it is found neither in the archaic alliterative verse of the Irish and Germanic peoples nor in classical
Greek and Latin poetry. It does however appear in the
rhetorical prose of the late empire—in the *Golden Ass* of
Apuleius as well as in the sermons of St. Augustine. A
primitive form occurs in some of the fifth century hymns.
But it is in Ireland that is seems to have been developed
to its fullest extent both in Latin and in the vernacular.[6]

Any reader, looking through the present collection, will
immediately see that Irish rhyme is not the same as the
rhyme used in English and in other languages. In fact,
what in English would be regarded as full rhyme, in Irish
would often be felt as a breach of good style. In Irish
rhyme the vowels, generally speaking, must be identical,
and the rhyming consonants must be of the same quality,
that is, broad or slender.[7] Furthermore, the Irish divided

---

6. 'Latin Poetry in Ireland' by Francis Byrne (in *Early
   Irish Poetry*, ed. James Carney, Mercier Press, 4 Bridge
   St., Cork, Ireland).
7. A broad consonant is a consonant preceded by *a, o,* or
   *u*; a slender consonant is a consonant preceded by *e,* or
   *i*. However, since Old and Middle Irish orthography is
   imprecise in this matter the reader without training

the consonants into six classes, and consonants, when single, rhyme only with others from the same class. The following are the classes:

I. Voiced stops: b, d, g. In these poems, in internal or final position, generally represented by p, t, c.

II. Voiceless stops: p, t, c; frequently, in internal or final position, represented by pp, tt, cc.

III. Voiceless spirants: ph (f), th, ch.

IV. Voiced spirants and weakly pronounced voiced liquids (in internal or final position): b (=v), m (=nasal v), d (=th, as in English 'then'), g (as in German 'morgen'), l, n, r.

V. Strongly pronounced voiced liquids: m (=mm, often so written), ll, nn, ng, rr. Consonants of this class, following a long vowel or diphthong, may rhyme with those of class IV.

VI. The consonant *s* (frequently written *ss*) rhymes only with itself.

The most characteristic Irish metre is called *deibide* (written *deibhidhe* in modern Irish, and pronounced *devee*). It may be useful for the reader to give a metrical analysis of a single verse (VII, p. 14):

> Sainemlu cech dóen a chruth,
> brestu cech sóer a balcbruth,
> gaíthiu cech bruinniu fo nim,
> fíriánu cech breithemain.

---

will not always recognise the quality of an Irish consonant. For instance, in modern Irish the word for woman is written *bean*, in Old Irish *ben:* in each case the quality of the final consonant is broad. In earlier Irish *bein* is written, when the final consonant is slender.

In this stanza there are seven syllables in each line; *chruth* rhymes with *balcbruth*, the final consonants being identical, from class III above; *nim* rhymes with *breithemain* (which could have been spelt *breithemin*). In Irish the accent normally falls heavily on the first syllable of a word. Hence, in this particular metre, rhyme is between a stressed (*chruth*) and an unstressed syllable (*-bruth*). The internal rhyme between *dóen* and *sóer* in the first couplet may be accidental.

This metre has many variations, one of which, for instance, is to have only three syllables in the first line (as in the third and fourth quatrains on page 34).

We may analyse another quatrain (XV, p. 30):

> Ó do-éctar mo láma
> ot é cnámacha cáela,
> nítat fíu turcbáil taccu
> súas tar na maccu cáema.

This quatrain is in a metre called *rannaigecht bec*. There are seven syllables in each line, and the endings are disyllabic, all of which can be expressed in the formula $7^2 + 7^2 + 7^2 + 7^2$. *cáela* rhymes with *cáema*, having an identical diphthong áe,[8] and *l* and *m* (=nazalized *v*) coming from the same consonantal class. *láma* is metrically related to *cáela* and *cáema* by a device called consonance, which is really a more subtle form of rhyme: it has all the requirements of rhyme, except that the accented vowel element need not be identical, but corresponds only in length: the *m* is from the same

---

8. This diphthong, expressed in later orthography by *ao*, is followed by a broad consonant.

consonantal class, is broad in quality, and the long vowel *á* balances the diphthong *áe*. There is internal rhyme between *taccu* and *maccu*. It is to be noted that of the twenty-eight syllables in the quatrain ten of them are controlled by the rhyming system.

A poem is not necessarily composed in stanzas of the same metre, and in the poem from which the above quatrain is taken there is considerable variation.

All except three of the Irish poems in the present collection are based on a count of syllables. The two modern poems VIII and XL are in stressed metres which, after an underground existence of some centuries, supplanted syllabic versification in the seventeenth century; poem XXXVIII is a passage from a saga, a piece of heightened prose, which I have thought worthy of dividing into lines and presenting as verse. This piece in some ways resembles the kind of poetry that preceded the stanzaic verse which forms the bulk of the present collection.

Poem I is the earliest in this collection, and in the notes I have shown how it was necessary to reconstruct the original from two defective sources: a seventh-century Latin translation and an Irish version from a late ninth-century life of St. Patrick. The line *Canfaid míchrabud*, missing in the Irish version, had to be based on the Latin *Incantabit nefas*. There is no doubt about *Canfaid*,[9] and *míchrabud* was a perfect rendering of *nefas* and had the advantage that it alliterated with *méis* in the following line. I felt quite happy about this rendering and regarded

---

9. The form, however, should probably be changed to *cechna*, the older form of the third singular future of *canaid*.

the poem as a piece in an archaic irregular metrical structure. But as the work went through the press I developed some doubts. In the first stanza (if we are justified in dividing the poem into stanzas) each line consists of four syllables and ends in a disyllable ($4^2 + 4^2 + 4^2 + 4^2$). In the second stanza, as the text stands, we have a pattern $5^3 + 8^2 + 8^2 + 4^2$. The word that I have reconstructed from the Latin, *míchrabud*, is odd man out in this arrangement, and consequently falls under grave suspicion. I would suggest here that we must seek further for an Irish word of two syllables that would translate *nefas*. This stanza would then have the metrical form $4^2 + 8^2 + 8^2 + 4^2$, and we might compare poem XXXVII in a well-known and popular metre based on the alternation of four and eight syllables.

## THE LATIN POEMS[10]

It will be useful to deal first with the Latin poems. II and III are included in some notes written in Latin by Bishop Tírechán towards the end of the seventh century. This bishop could hardly write a sentence in Latin without allowing his native Gaelic idiom to show through, so we may reasonably conclude that these poems must have existed before his time. I have dated them to about 600 A.D., perhaps a little earlier, about which time the first efforts were being made to present material relative to the life of St. Patrick, who had died in 493.[11] III, St.

---

10. References to sources and to earlier discussions of particular poems will be found in the notes.
11. *The Problem of St. Patrick*, James Carney, Dublin, 1961, pp. 131-4.

Patrick's Creed, purports to be the saint's own work—I will leave it to those better versed in St. Patrick's curious Latinity to say whether or not this could be so. But if it is not so, it could be an early versification of a creed which Patrick taught during his mission to the Irish.

St. Columbanus, author of IV (not to be confused with his contemporary, St. Columcille), is one of the earliest of the Irish Latinists whose work has survived in any quantity. He came to the Continent from Ireland about 591. He lived at first in Merovingian Gaul, busied himself with religion, poetry and politics, with the latter so indiscreetly that he had perforce to move to northern Italy. Here, in the land of his second exile, he founded under an Irish rule the monastery of Bobbio, which came to be his most famous foundation. The poem which I translate has been frequently regarded as a boat-song. It is rather, I think, a poetic exhortation to his monks to persevere to the end, with an image drawn from the boat, that by the effort of its crew passes through storm and tempest to the ultimate security of port.

Sedulius Scottus (author of XIX-XXIV) at Christmas about the year 845 arrived on the Continent from Ireland and sought out Hartgar, bishop of Liège. Sedulius has left a great collection of his Latin verse. Those selected for translation here show his career from the day of his arrival until about thirteen years later when, we may presume, he either died or returned to Ireland. He was immediately put in charge of the cathedral school by Hartgar, and we shortly find four other Irishmen employed there. These, who probably include his two initial companions, Sedulius calls 'four charioteers of the Lord, lights of the Irish race.' All through his poems he emphasizes his nationality, and demands that as one who has suffered exile from his own country he be given nothing but the best.[12] Hence his demands for a good table (XXI) and a house safe from robbers and decorated in the most modern style (XX).

In Sedulius's verse we get a very good idea of his conception of the world. It was bounded by India on one side, by Ireland on the other. He was conscious of the Slavs and the Scythians at the extremities of Europe and the margins of Asia, of the Holy Land, Aethiopia, Libya, and the whole ancient world dominated by Romans, Greeks and Hebrews. His immediate world is Italy, especially Rome, and western Europe inhabited by Germans, Franks and Irish. He sees this group being menaced on the south by the Moors and Saracens, and on the opposite side by the heathen Northmen. Poem XXII is a hymn of thanks for a victory gained by Hartgar over the latter—we can compare poem X, written in Irish at the same period and expressing fear of the same enemy.

XXIII is an extract from a much longer poem. Hartgar had promised Sedulius a present of a ram. But before the beast was transferred from the episcopal to the scholastic field, a thief entered the palace grounds. Dogs were set on him—the thief escaped, but the dogs killed the ram.

Sedulius made a long mock-heroic poem about the death of this innocent beast. In what now might seem somewhat dubious taste, he makes a comparison between Christ, the Lamb of God, and the slain ram. Christ died

---

12. The theme of exile is a constant one in Irish poetry from the earliest period. Typical is XXXV, a dramatic poem, put in the mouth of Colum Cille.

for sinners, the innocent ram died for the thief. The lines translated here are indirectly autobiographical, for Sedulius praises the ram for the lack of those very faults which he knew to be conspicuously his own, loquaciousness, love of meat, drink and high society.

These poems of Sedulius, light and personal, give no adequate idea of his accomplishment. He was a social personality, the friend of emperors and high ecclesiastics. But he had gained his position in society by sound and solid scholastic work. He busied himself with Latin grammar and wrote commentaries on the grammatical works of Eutyches and Priscian. He composed a commentary on the gospel of Matthew and another on the epistles of St. Paul. Amongst the works which he had brought from Ireland was a copy of a text called *Proverbia Graecorum* which appears to have been written in Ireland as early as the sixth century.

His most original work was *De Rectoribus Christianis* 'Concerning Christian Rulers,' a treatise on the duties of a prince. This was written for Lothar II, son to the emperor Lothar I. It deals partly with the problem of relations between Church and State, and is regarded as an important contribution to the development of political thought in the Middle Ages. The work is written in prose, but every section is recapitulated in verse. This form of writing was to become increasingly popular in Irish, but we cannot maintain that Sedulius was here following Irish models; he is imitating the form of *De Consolatione Philosophiae* by Boethius.

In form the Latin poems of Sedulius are Carolingian verse of a very high order of competence. Whether or not it will eventually emerge that there is in it any significant

Gaelic element I cannot say. In his poem on the defeat of the Northmen Sedulius reckons the numbers of the slain. He says (as I translate him): 'Count not unknown, count not the menials, on that dread field lay bloody there three times ten thousand.' This, of course, must be ridiculous exaggeration, and as such quite Irish. Typical, however, of the Irish aristocratic attitude to battles is to reckon the numbers of people of some quality who fell, and to dismiss the *daescurshluag* or 'rabble' losses as something of no account.

It is, I would say, almost certain that Sedulius would have written verse in Irish as well as in Latin. There is in the Royal Library of Dresden a Greek text of the thirteen epistles of St. Paul with a Latin interlinear version. The manuscript belongs to the circle of Sedulius. It reflects one of Sedulius's own particular interests, the epistles of St. Paul; the writer knew Greek, as did Sedulius, and amongst other marginalia it contains the names of Hartgar, and of Gunthar, bishop of Cologne, to both of whom Sedulius had written poems. The great medievalist Traube had little hesitation in attributing this manuscript to Sedulius himself. As marginalia in this manuscript there are some quatrains in Irish, including the clever and slightly cynical comment on pilgrimages to Rome which is poem XXXII in the present collection. This quatrain may very well have been composed by Sedulius; it has the epigrammatic quality one would expect from him.

Like any other intelligent man, despite some superficial appearances to the contrary, Sedulius was essentially humble. He could boldly declare his talents, but see their insignificance in universal terms. It is a sign of his humility that, loquacious as he was, he could still sum up a life rich in achievement in the six lines of verse that constitute poem XXIV.

In the introduction to *Ancient Irish Poetry* Kuno Meyer has written: 'In Nature Poetry the Gaelic muse may vie with that of any other nation. Indeed, these poems occupy a unique position in the literature of the world. To seek out and watch and love Nature, in its tiniest phenomena as in its grandest, was given to no people so early and so fully as to the Celt. Many hundreds of Gaelic and Welsh poems testify to this fact. It is a characteristic of these poems that in none of them do we get an elaborate or sustained description of any scene or scenery, but rather a succession of pictures and images, which the poet, like an impressionist, calls up before us by light and skilful touches. Like the Japanese, the Celts were always quick to take an artistic hint; they avoid the obvious and the commonplace; the half-said thing to them is dearest.'

There are a number of poems here that illustrate Meyer's statement, VI, XI, XVI, XXVII, XXXIV. Indeed, poem XVI resembles somewhat the Japanese *haiku*. A poem, similar in metre and spirit, inadvertently omitted from the collection, may be given here:

| | |
|---|---|
| Int én bec | The little bird |
| ro léic feit | has whistled |
| do rind guip | from point of beak |
| glanbuide; | bright yellow; |
| fo-ceird faíd | sends a cry |
| os Loch Laíg | over Loch Laíg |

xx

| lon do chraíb | blackbird from branch |
| chrannmuige.[13] | in wooded plain. |

These poems emerge from a Christian society that, at its height, was perhaps the most ascetic that Western Europe has known. The flesh and the Devil were firmly rejected, but the grimness of life was tempered by an acceptance of the beauty of the world, of nature and animal life, as the handicraft of God. There were moments of rebellion when life seemed too hard to bear, and there were doubtless many backsliders. A distinguished Harvard professor has translated the Irish epitaph of the eighth-century monk Cú Cuimne from whose Latin hymn to the Virgin Mary we have already quoted above. I have not seen the translation in print, but simply heard it passed from mouth to mouth and quote it from memory:

> Cú Chuimne in his youth
> read his way through half the truth;
> he let the other half lie
> and gave women a try.
>
> Good for him, in his old age
> he became a full sage;
> he gave women the laugh
> and read the other half.

Sometimes the grim asceticism was relieved by a resort to a wry humour. In a poem written about 1000 A.D. a poet, unfortunately anonymous, puts himself in the dock

---

13. Cf. Murphy, *Early Irish Lyrics*, p. 6.

on a charge of allowing his mind to wander in strange and unseemly places during the singing of the psalms. Indeed, it is possible that the poem formed in his mind during one of the long periods of community prayer, and would thus be part of the substance of his sin:

> Is mebul dom imrádud
> a méit élas úaimm
> ad-águr a imgábud
> i lló brátha búain . . .[14]

> A shame on my thinking
> how it wanders away;
> it will cause me embarrassment
> on Last Judgement day.

> At psalm time it rushes forth
> on a pathway that's odd,
> running, raving, misbehaving
> in the presence of God.

> To merry women's company,
> the unvirtuous kind,
> through wood and through cities
> faster than the wind.

> When road is smooth it travels
> merrily and gay,
> but passes just as easily
> the impenetrable way.

---

14. For the Irish text see Murphy, *Early Irish Lyrics*, p. 38.

It needs no ship to journey
   and the seas go by,
jumps with but a single leap
   from solid earth to sky.

No course of wisdom does it run
   whether near or far
and after all foolishness
   it's back where we are.

Put a fetter on its leg,
   chain it to prayer?
Yes! But in a minute's time
   it's no longer there.

Little use in beating it,
   plying whip or rod:
like an eel's tail it slips away
   from my grasp and from God.

No chain and no dark dungeon
   will hinder its course;
it laughs at seas and fortresses
   is mocking of force.

Dear Christ, lord of chastity,
   chain thinking in place
with power of spirit septiform
   and all His grace.

Make, great elemental God,
   the heart be still,

that you be my only love
and I your will.

May I come to Christ at last
and then to see
that He is no unsteady thing,
not wandering, like me.

Poem XV, which I have called 'Ebbing' is somewhat of a mystery.[15] It has been taken as a dramatic lyric, a presentation in Christian dress of the Hag of Beare, who was in all probability a pagan mythological figure. Before translating this poem I spent some five months reading it with a seminar class, making a fresh examination of the manuscript tradition, and questioning where necessary the hitherto accepted interpretation of phrases, lines and quatrains. The seminar, which was held for one hour weekly, included amongst other distinguished scholars the late Frank O'Connor, the famous Irish short-story writer who was particularly fascinated by this poem. During this study many subtleties and nuances became apparent. The poem is probably ninth century. It is not, in my opinion, a 'dramatic lyric.' When the author says, 'I am the hag of Buí and Beare (*Is mé caillech Bérri Buí*) what is meant is "In my condition, outliving those I love, I resemble the old hag of Beare who lived through seven

15. An Irish lyric poem has no title—it is usually quoted by its first line. This poem has been generally known as 'The Lament of the Hag of Beare.' I have deliberately departed from the usual title, which, it seems to me, somewhat prejudices the interpretation.

ages." The poem continues as a passionate statement of
the poet's own dilemma, having outlived youth and beauty
and being mercilessly thrown into an asceticism to which
her intellect acceded, but against which every other
natural instinct rebelled. Although I say 'her' I am anything but sure that the poem was written by a woman.
In an essay on the Irish bardic poet, to be published
shortly, I have pointed out how Irish bardic poets, when
praising their princely or royal patrons, could assume,
through a well-established conceit, the completely
feminine role of 'king-lover.' I have written there: 'It
could be maintained, but perhaps not with certainty, that
one of the finest poems of this type is the ninth-century
poem in which the poet speaks in the character of the
Old Woman of Beare. The poet, in such an interpretation,
was what one may call a "king-lover": when old age was
approaching he took unwillingly to religion; he expresses
all his past experiences with kings in the person of an
old harlot who, after a good spring, summer and autumn,
found herself rejected by her patrons in the early months
of her winter.'

It may, however, be preferable to take the poem at its
face value, that is, as having been written by a woman.[16]
There was an Irish queen, Gormlaith, who died in 946.

---

16. Outside the monastic milieu poetry in Ireland was
    written largely by hereditary professional poets.
    Líadan, to whom poem XIII is attributed, is presented
    in the saga from which the poem is taken, as a
    professional woman poet. There is also every reason
    to believe that in the ninth century an educated or
    aristocratic lady might make a habit of composing
    verse.

Her father was king of Tara and of Ireland. She married successively three kings, Cerball, king of Leinster, Cormac, king of Munster, and finally Níall Glúndub, king of Ireland. Later she became a figure in romance, giving rise to a tale 'The love of Gormlaith for Níall Glúdub.' Finally in her old age she retired to a convent. Gormlaith can hardly be the writer of this poem: the geographical references suggest strongly that the writer belonged to what is now the county of Tipperary,[17] and it might be difficult, on purely linguistic grounds, to suggest as late a date as 940. But the poem could have been written by an aristocratic woman of somewhat earlier date, whose experiences were somewhat similar to those of Gormlaith. Indeed, with the system of dynastic intermarriage, and the frequent early death of men of the princely warrior caste, the pattern of Gormlaith's marriages would not be unusual. It is doubtful that we shall ever achieve a satisfactory solution of this problem.

I have mentioned above the title of a saga 'The love of Gormlaith for Níall Glúndub.' The very title raises another matter relevant to some of these poems. In early Ireland, in direct contrast to the present age, it may be said that the man and not the woman is the primary love-object. Hence, in early Irish literature, it is more usual to read of the tragic or unrequited love of a woman for a man, rather than the contrary. This is a reflection of life as it was. Irish warrior society, like early Greek society, tended to be male-orientated. Women in sages frequently make

---

17. Although Gormlaith, as wife of a king of Cashel, knew this area, she could hardly write such a poem without references to Tara or the northern part of Ireland.

their first and natural entry into a love-situation while serving food and drink to the men-folk. Hence we experience the tragedy of love in the suffering of Deirdre and of Gráinne—it is their natural destiny to outlive the warriors they loved. So in poem XII, the wife of Aed mac Ainmirech, king of Tara, remembers him when he is dead. In poem XIII Líadan remembers Cuirithir when he has left her; in XXXVIII we read, in a poetic passage from a saga, of Findabair's passionate remembrance of a single moment in her life when the beauty of her dead lover Fróech was revealed to her.

Most early Irish poetry is anonymous. In the late period that is, from about 1250 onwards, the authorship of a poem is generally stated. To this class belongs XXXVII by Gofraidh Fionn Ó Dálaigh, an excerpt from a longer poem. The poem was written about 1354, and describes, in allegorical terms drawn from Irish mythology, the visit of the poet's patron, Maurice FitzMaurice, to the court of the English king in London.

Poem XXV, two stanzas on India, are an extract from a longer work on world geography—verse was used in Ireland to teach any and every subject. The author, Airbertach mac Cosse, who died towards the close of the tenth century, was fer léiginn or chief professor at the monastery of Ros Ailithir (now Ros Carbery in Co. Cork). He was probably the author of Saltair na Rann, the Psalter of Quatrains, a versification of biblical history, one of the most ambitious poems in early Irish.

Máel Ísu Ó Brolcháin, author of XXIX and XXXI, lived throughout the greater part of the eleventh century and died in 1086. Poem XXIX is anonymous in the manuscripts and the reasons for ascribing it to Máel Ísu are discussed elsewhere.[18] The poem at one time gave rise to much comment and theorizing. The name Crínóc is a woman's name, or could be used as such, and means 'Dear little old thing.' Kuno Meyer, who first discovered and published this poem, accepted the poem quite literally, despite difficulties which must be apparent even to a casual reader. He assigned it, on no very good grounds, to the tenth century. Crínóc, he held, was one of those religious women who contracted spiritual marriage (*Geistige Ehe*) with clerics or ascetics of the opposite sex, and he adduced this poem to prove that this custom, suppressed in the Church generally by the council of Nicea in the fourth century, lived on in Ireland until the tenth.

For me the poem always constituted a problem, for Meyer's interpretation, unlikely on the face of it, left too many questions unanswered. But the problem lay upon my mind for many years before the easy and natural solution suggested itself: it was a poem written by a religious in his old age to an old and tattered copy of the Psalms which had been his first lesson book. The solution, which has found general acceptance by scholars, emerged quite clearly when I noted that in early Ireland a boy destined for the Church began his education at the age of seven, and that the Psalter, from which he learned Latin, reading, singing and religion, was his first lesson book. This book, which he had used in his youth in its virgin freshness passed through four generations of young scholars before by some chance it came back into the old priest's hands again.

---

18. See Notes for references.

XVIII, the poem on Fate, is worth some comment. The text was discovered and published by me some twenty-five years ago. It belongs to about the year 900, or perhaps a little later. It is interesting as an exemplification of Irish views on fate and destiny current over a thousand years ago, and, as we shall see, persisting down to modern times. Stanza 6 of this poem, translated quite literally, says: 'It does not stop me from setting out on a journey that someone in a gathering sneezes—the sod on which my tomb-stone has been shaped, I must needs approach it.'

From classical antiquity, down through the middle ages, a sneeze was always considered a bad omen. To avert the evil, in Germany and America, one still says 'Gesundheit'; in Irish one says 'Dia linn,' 'God be with us.' The sod of death idea, however, is so far as I know, confined to Ireland, Iceland and Sweden.[19]

The Irish had a curious belief that for everybody there existed three 'sods' or spots: the 'sod of birth,' the 'sod of death,' and the 'sod of burial.' Each sod was predestined, the sod of burial having its importance in being the pre-destined place of personal resurrection on the Last Day. The sod of death (which may originally have been the same as the sod of burial) came to be thought of in the folk mind as a particular piece of earth somewhere in the world upon which a man one day would tread, and the moment of contact would be that of his death. The

---

19. See an article by Maura Carney, *Arv*, Journal of Scandinavian Folklore, Vol. 13, 1957, pp. 157 ff., Anne Holtsmark, *Lochlann*, Vol. 2, 1962, pp. 122 - 7.

sod seems to beckon each and everyone on, and belief in it still survives in Irish folklore. A common type of folktale tells how a man discovered what was destined to be his sod of death, had it safely, as he thought, disposed of, thrown to the bottom of the sea or otherwise destroyed. But by some wonderful or unexpected circumstance, at the predestined moment, the sod would find its place beneath his feet.

The following is a translation of a passage from a statement written in Irish in 1945 by a 68-year-old Irish-speaker from Doolin, Co. Clare, on the beliefs of the people in his district concerning fate and destiny.

'I wish to mention the belief that the old people had that it was laid out for a person from the time the crown of his head came into the world where his sod of death was. For this person it was laid out that for him, or for her, the side of the road would be as a sod of death, for another the middle of the field, or out on the brown mountain, or in the loneliness of the wood, or—God save us from the danger!—a person could have as sod of death a violent death.

I remember when a poor girl from this town fell down a terrible cliff over there a dozen years ago, what an old neighbour, no longer living for many a day, said. There were droves of people from the towns around present, everywhere taking the full of their eyes fearfully of the poor dead thing who was thrown there on a fissure in the cliff hundreds of feet from the top. This person and that were trying to ease in some way the torment of the girl's father, but what the old man I mentioned had to say when he looked down at the dreadful sight was: "'Twas her sod of death that was there" (*Sé fód a báis do bhí ann*).'[20]

We may now make some comment on poem VII which consists of extracts from a much longer poem. Some years ago in the National Library of Ireland I was fortunate enough to come upon twenty-three pages of Irish verse which by a curious mischance had not hitherto come under the notice of scholars. Though the manuscript was seventeenth century, the verse was some nine hundred years earlier; the greater part of it was by a poet who was unknown save for his name: Blathmac son of Cú Brettan son of Congus. Blathmac was of the Fir Rois; in other words he came from an area covering parts of the counties of Louth and Monaghan. His father, who was king of the Fir Rois, had some part in the battle of Allen in 722 and died in 740. His brother Donn Bó died about 759, so we can reasonably date these poems to somewhere in the second half of the eighth century. The discovery of such a significant quantity of early verse illustrates the fact that, owing to the lack of sufficient trained workers in the field, the literature of Ireland in the early centuries is still an incompletely known subject.

Finally it remains to make some comment on the arrangement of these poems. This is only roughly chronological, the chronological factor being frequently ignored in the interests of an interesting juxtaposition. The first poem fittingly introduces Christian Gaelic Ireland and announces the death of paganism. The last, written in the seventeenth century when the Gaelic

---

20. As translated by Maura Carney, loc. cit.

social order had received its death blow, is a somewhat bitter appeal to Irish traditionalist scholars to forget their disputes about the mythical and historical past and by implication to face the hard realities of the present.

As a last word I may point out what by now must be obvious to the reader: many of the poems are poems with which as a scholar I had a particular association. It will not be equally obvious that sometimes a poem was translated because it seemed at one point or another in my life to have relevance to my own experience or feeling.

JAMES CARNEY

*Dublin Institute for Advanced Studies*
*University of California, Los Angeles*
December 3rd, 1966.

# MEDIEVAL IRISH LYRICS

# I

## Ticfa Tálcenn

Ticfa Tálcenn
tar muir mercenn,
a thí thollcenn,
a chrann crombcenn.

Canfaid míchrábud
a méis i n-airthiur a thige;
fris-gérat a muinter uile:
'Amén, Amén.'


# II

## Quis Est Deus?

Quis est Deus
et ubi est Deus
et cuius est Deus
et ubi habitaculum eius?

Si habet filios et filias,
aurum et argentum, Deus vester?

Si vivus semper,
si pulcher,
si filium eius
nutrierunt multi?

2

# I

## Adze-head

Across the sea will come Adze-head,
crazed in the head,
his cloak with hole for the head,
his stick bent in the head.

He will chant impiety
from a table in the front of his house;
all his people will answer:
'Be it thus. Be it thus.'

# II

## The Questions Of Ethne Alba

Who is God
and where is God,
of whom is God,
and where His dwelling?

Has He sons and daughters,
gold and silver, this God of yours?

Is He ever-living,
is He beautiful,
was His son
fostered by many?

3

Si filiae eius
carae et pulchrae sunt
hominibus mundi?

Si in caelo
an in terra est?
In aequore,
in fluminibus,
in montanis,
in convallibus?

Dic nobis
notitiam eius:
Quomodo videbitur,
quomodo diligitur,
quomodo invenitur?

Si in iuventute,
si in senectute
invenitur?


# III

## Deus Noster

Deus noster, Deus omnium hominum,
Deus caeli ac terrae, maris et fluminum,
deus solis ac lunae, omnium siderum,
Deus montium sublimium, valliumque humilium,
Deus super caelo et in caelo et sub caelo.

Are His daughters
dear and beautiful
to the men of the world?

Is He in heaven
or on the earth?
In the sea,
in the rivers,
in the mountains,
in the valleys?

Speak to us
tidings of Him:
How will He be seen,
how is He loved,
how is He found?

Is it in youth
or is it in old age
He is found?


# III

## St. Patrick's Creed

Our God, God of all men,
God of heaven and earth, sea and rivers,
God of sun and moon, of all the stars,
God of high mountains and of lowly valleys,
God over heaven, and in heaven, and under heaven.

Habet habitaculum
erga caelum et terram et mare
et omnia quae sunt in eis.

Inspirat omnia,
vivificat omnia,
superat omnia,
suffulcit omnia.

Solis lumen inluminat,
lumen noctis et notitias vallat
et fontes fecit in arida terra
et insolas in mari siccas
et stellas in ministerium
maiorum luminum posuit.

Filium habet
coaeternum sibi et consimilem sibi;
non iunior Filius Patri
nec Pater Filio senior.

Et Spiritus Sanctus
inflat in eis;
non separantur Pater
et Filius et Spiritus Sanctus.

He has a dwelling
in heaven and earth and sea
and in all things that are in them.

He inspires all things,
He quickens all things,
He is over all things,
He supports all things.

He makes the light of the sun to shine,
He surrounds the moon and stars,
and He has made wells in the arid earth,
placed dry islands in the sea
and stars for the service
of the greater luminaries.

He has a Son
coeternal with Himself, like to Himself;
not junior is Son to Father,
nor Father senior to the Son.

And the Holy Spirit
breathes in them;
not separate are Father
and Son and Holy Spirit.

# IV

## En Silvis Caesa

En, silvis caesa fluctu meat acta carina
Bicornis Rheni et pelagus perlabitur uncta.
  *Heia viri! nostrum reboans echo sonet heia!*

Extollunt venti flatus, nocet horridus imber,
Sed vis apta virum superat sternitque procellam.
  *Heia viri! nostrum reboans echo sonet heia!*

Nam cedunt nimbi studio, ceditque procella,
cuncta domat nisus, labor improbus omnia vincit.
  *Heia viri! nostrum reboans echo sonet heia!*

Durate et vosmet rebus servate secundis,
O passi graviora, dabit deus his quoque finem.
  *Heia viri! nostrum reboans echo sonet heia!*

Sic inimicus agit invisus corda fatigans,
Ac male temptando quatit intima corda furore.
  *Vestra, viri, Christum memorans niens personet heia!*

State animo fixi, hostisque spernite strofas,
Virtutum vosmet armis defendite rite.
  *Vestra, viri, Christum memorans mens personet heia!*

# IV

## Columbanus To His Monks

See, cut in woods, through flood of twin-horned Rhine
passes the keel, and greased slips over seas —
*Heave, men! And let resounding echo sound our 'heave'.*

The winds raise blasts, wild rain-storms wreak their spite
but ready strength of men subdues it all —
*Heave, men! And let resounding echo sound our 'heave'.*

Clouds melt away and the harsh tempest stills,
effort tames all, great toil is conqueror —
*Heave, men! And let resounding echo sound our 'heave'.*

Endure and keep yourselves for happy things;
you suffered worse, and these too God shall end —
*Heave, men! And let resounding echo sound our 'heave'.*

Thus acts the foul fiend: wearing out the heart
and with temptation shaking inmost parts —
*You men, remember Christ with mind still sounding
'heave'.*

Stand firm in soul and spurn the foul fiend's tricks
and seek defence in virtue's armoury —
*You men, remember Christ with mind still sounding
'heave'.*

Firma fides cuncta superat studiumque beatum,
Hostis et antiquus cedens sua spicula frangit.
*Vestra, viri, Christum memorans mens personet heia!*


Rex quoque virtutum, rerum fons, summa potestas,
Certanti spondet, vincenti praemia donat.
*Vestra, viri, Christum memorans mens personet heia!*




# V

## Is Mebul

Is mebul
élúd Ríg na fírinne
ocus chairte fri demun.




# VI

## Scél Lemm Dúib

Scél lemm dúib:
dordaid dam,
snigid gaim,
ro-fáith sam;

Firm faith will conquer all and blessed zeal
and the old fiend yielding breaks at last his darts—
　*You men, remember Christ with mind still sounding*
　*'heave'.*

Supreme, of virtues King, and fount of things,
He promises in strife, gives prize in victory —
　*You men, remember Christ with mind still sounding*
　*'heave'.*


# V

## God And The Devil

It's evil
to shun the King of righteousness
and make compact with demon.


# VI

## Winter

News I bring:
bells the stag,
winter snow,
summer past;

gáeth ard úar,
ísel grían,
gair a rith,
ruirthech rían;

rorúad rath,
ro-cleth cruth,
ro-gab gnáth
giugrann guth;

ro-gab úacht
etti én,
aigre ré:
é mo scél.

# VII

## Tair Cucum, a Maire Boíd

BLATHMAC MAC CON BRETTAN

Tair cucum, a Maire boíd,
do choíniuth frit do rochoím;
dirsan dul fri croich dot mac
ba mind már, ba masgérat.

Co tochmurr frit mo di láim
ar do macind irgabáil:
Ísu con-atoí do brú,
nícon fochmai th'ógai-siu.

\* \* \*

wind high and cold,
low the sun,
short its course,
seas run strong;

russet bracken,
shape awry,
wild goose raises
wonted cry;

cold lays hold
on wings of bird,
icy time:
this I heard.

# VII

## To Mary And Her Son
BLATHMAC SON OF CÚ BRETTAN

Come to me, loving Mary,
that I may keen with you your very dear one;
Alas! The going to the cross of your son,
that great jewel, that beautiful champion.

That with you I may beat my two hands
for your fair son's captivity.
Your womb has conceived Jesus —
it has not marred your virginity.

\* \* \*

Cotn-abairt cen phecath fir,
do-forsat cen chneid ngalair;
rot-nert cen chumaid — cain rath! —
isind aimsir hi crochad.

Cair, in cúalaid mac am-ne
con-meseth a tréde-se?
Ní tuidchid for lesa ban
ocus nícon gignethar.

Prímgein Dé Athar fri nem
do mac, a Maire ingen;
ro-láithreth hi combairt glain
tri rath spirto sechtndelbaig.

Nícon fúair athair samlai,
a Maire, do macamrai;
ferr fáith, fisidiu cech druí,
rí ba hepscop, ba lánsuí.

Sainemlu cech dóen a chruth,
brestu cech sóer a balcbruth,
gaíthiu cech bruinniu fo nim,
fíriánu cech breithemain.

Maisiu, meldchu, mó macaib;
ó boí ina becbrataib
ru-fes a ndo-regad de,
gein tesairgne sochuide.

You have conceived him and no sin with man,
you brought him forth without ailing wound;
without grief he strengthened you (fair grace!)
at the time of his crucifixion.

I ask: Have you heard of a son like this,
one who could do these three things?
Such has not come upon the thighs of women
and such will not be born.

The first-begotten of God, the Father, in heaven
is your son, Mary, virgin;
he was begotten in a pure conception
through the power of the septiform Spirit.

No father has found, Mary,
the like of your renowned son;
better he than prophet, wiser than druid,
a king who was bishop and full sage.

His form was finer than that of other beings,
his stout vigour greater than any craftsman's,
wiser he than any breast under heaven,
juster than any judge.

More beautiful, more pleasant, bigger than other boys
since he was in his swaddling clothes;
it was known what would come of him,
a being for the saving of multitudes.

Sóer a ngein ro-génair úait,
rot-rath, a Maire, mórbúaid;
Críst mac Dé Athar do nim,
é ron-ucais i mBeithil.

*    *    *

Rom-bet mo théor aicdi lat,
a Maire mass muingelnat;
at-ethae, a grian na mban,
ót mac conid-midethar.

Mo buith for bith comba sen
la fíadait follnas rindnem,
ocus fáilte frium iar sin
isin mbithflaith mbithsuthain.

Cech óen díamba figel se
fo lige ocus éirge
ar imdídnad dianim tall
amail lúirech co cathbarr.

Cách nod-géba do cach deilb
i troscud aidchi Sathairnn
acht rob fo déraib cen meth,
a Maire, níb ifernach.

Fri tuidecht do maic co feirc
cona chroich fria ais imdeirc,
ara soírthar lat in tan
nach carae nod-coínfedar.

Noble the being born from you!
You were granted, Mary, a great gift:
Christ, son of the Father in heaven,
him have you borne in Bethlehem.

*       *       *

May I have from you my three petitions,
beautiful Mary, little white-necked one;
get them, sun amongst women,
from your son who has them in his power.

That I may be in the world till old
serving the Lord who rules starry heaven,
and that then there be a welcome for me
into the eternal, ever-enduring kingdom.

That everyone who uses this as a vigil prayer
at lying down and at rising,
that it may protect him from blemish in the other world
like a breastplate and helmet.

Everyone of any sort who shall recite it
fasting on Friday night,
provided only that it be with full-flowing tears,
Mary, may he not be for hell.

When your son comes in anger
with his cross on his reddened back,
that then you will save
any friend who shall have keened him.

Airiut, a Maire co llí,
rega-sa i n-aitiri:
cách gébas in coíniud nglan
ra-mbiä a thuarastal.

Dot-gaur co foclaib fíraib,
a Maire, a maisrígain,
con roirem cobrai ma tú
do airchisecht do chridi-siu.

Conro-choíner Críst as glé
frit-su tucht bas n-incride,
a lie lógmar laindrech,
a máthair in mórchoimdeth.

Ce chon-messinn co cach rían
doíni betho fo móenmíad
do-regtis lim ocus lat
conro-choíntis do rígmac.

Do lámchomairt cen moraich
mnáib macaib ferolaib
conro-choíntis for cach dind
ríg do-rósat cach n-óenrind.

Nacha cumgaim; ciche féin
do mac frit-su co daigléir
acht do-dichis-siu nach ré
do chélidiu cucum-sae.

For you, beautiful Mary,
I shall go as guarantor:
anyone who says the full keen,
he shall have his reward.

I call you with true words,
Mary, beautiful queen,
that we may have talk together
to pity your heart's darling.

So that I may keen the bright Christ
with you in the most heartfelt way,
shining precious jewel,
mother of the great Lord.

Were I rich and honoured
ruling the people of the world to every sea,
they would all come with you and me
to keen your royal son.

There would be beating of hands
by women, children and men,
that they might keen on every hill-top
the king who made every star.

I cannot do this. With heartfelt feeling
I will bewail your son with you
if only you come at some time
on a visit to me.

Do airchisecht chridi cen on
con roirem ar ndiabor,
a chond na creitme glaine,
tair cucum, a boídMaire.


# VIII

## Caoineadh Na Maighdine

'Is mithid dom', arsan Mhaighdean, 'dul ag fiosrú mo
    ghrádh geal'
        (Och! Ochón agus ochón ó).
Do bhí a ceann scaoilte is a cosa gan náda
        (Och! Ochón agus ochón ó),
isí ag bailiú a chuid fola ós cionn an fhásaigh
        (Och! Ochón agus ochón ó).


Do léim sí isteach is amach thar ghárda
        (Och! Ochón agus ochón ó).
'Dia dhuit, a mhic, nó an aithnid duit do mháthair'
        (Och! Ochón agus ochón ó).
'Bíodh agat an fhoidhne agus geobhaidh tú na grásta'
        (Och! Ochón agus ochón ó).
'A leinbh, is mór é t'ualach is leig cuid de ar do mháthair'
        (Och! Ochón agus ochón ó).
'Iomchruigheadh gach n-aon a chrosa féin agus
    iomchróchad-sa thar ceann sliocht Adhaimh é'
        (Och! Ochón agus ochón ó).

Come to me, loving Mary,
you, head of unsullied faith,
that we may have talk together
with the compassion of unblemished heart.


# VIII

## The Virgin's Lament

Said the Virgin: 'Let me go to be with my bright darling'
        (Och! Ochone and Ochone O).
Her hair was flying and her feet were bare
        (Och! Ochone and Ochone O),
and she gathering his blood in the desert place
        (Och! Ochone and Ochone O).


She sprang in and out through the guarding soldiers
        (Och! Ochone and Ochone O).
'Bless you my son, do you know your own mother?'
        (Och! Ochone and Ochone O).
'Have patience, mother and you will get all graces'
        (Och! Ochone and Ochone O).
'O child, it's a heavy burden, let your mother part bear it'
        (Och! Ochone and Ochone O).
'To each his own cross, for me that of Adam's children'
        (Och! Ochone and Ochone O).

# IX

## Dom-farcai Fidbaidæ Fál

Dom-farcai fidbaidæ fál,
    fom-chain loíd luin — lúad nad cél;
húas mo lebrán, ind línech,
    fom-chain trírech inna n-én.

Fomm-chain coí menn — medair mass —
    hi mbrot glass de dindgnaib doss.
Débrad! nom-choimmdiu coíma,
    caín-scríbaimm fo foída ross.


# X

## Is Acher In Gáith In-Nocht

Is acher in gáith in-nocht,
fu-fúasna fairggæ findfolt:
ní ágor réimm mora minn
dond láechraid lainn úa Lothlind.


# XI

## Fuitt Co Bráth

Fuitt co bráth!
    Is mó in doinenn ar cách;
is ob cach etriche án,
    ocus is loch lán cach áth.

# IX

## Writing Out Of Doors

A wall of forest looms above
    and sweetly the blackbird sings;
all the birds make melody
    over me and my books and things.

There sings to me the cuckoo
    from bush-citadels in grey hood.
God's doom! May the Lord protect me
    writing well, under the great wood.


# X

## The Vikings

Bitter and wild is the wind to-night
tossing the tresses of the sea to white.
On such a night as this I feel at ease:
fierce Northmen only course the quiet seas.


# XI

## Forever Cold

Forever cold!
Weather grim and grimmer still,
glittering brook a river
and ford a brimming lake.

Is méit muir mór cech loch lonn,
　　is drong cech cuire gúr gann,
méit taul scéith banna dond linn,
　　méit moltchrocann finn cech slamm.

Méit cuithe cach lathrach léig,
　　coirthe cach réid, caill cach móin,
inna helta, nís tá dín,
　　snechtae finn fír do-roich tóin.

Ro-íad réod rótu gribb
　　iar ngléo glicc im choirthi Cuilt,
con-gab doinenn dar cach leth
　　coná apair nech acht 'Fuitt'.


# XII
## Batar Inmuini Trí Toíb

Batar inmuini trí toíb
　　frisná fresciu aitherrech,
tóebán Temro, toíb Taillten,
　　toíb Áedo maicc Ainmirech.


# XIII
## Cen Áinius

Cen áinius
in gním í do-rigénus,
an ro-carus ro-cráidius.

The lake a great sea
(each meagre band a company)
rain-drop like shield-boss
and snow-flake like wether-skin.

The dirty puddle is a great pit,
level land is risen, the moor a wood,
no shelter for the flocks of birds
and white snow reaches up to haunch.

Sudden frost has closed the roads
encircling with cunning the standing-stone at Colt;
grim weather lies entrenched on every side
and no one utters anything but: 'Cold'.

## XII
### Áed Mac Ainmirech

Beloved were three sides
I cannot hope to see again,
side of Tara, side of Tailltiu,
side of Áed mac Ainmirech.

## XIII
### Líadan's Lament

No pleasure
that deed I did, tormenting him,
tormenting what I treasure.

Ba mire
nád dernad a airer-som
mainbed ómun ríg nime.

Níbu amlos
dó-som in dál dúthracair,
ascnam sech phéin i Pardos.

Bec mbríge
ro-chráidi frimm Cuirithir,
fris-sium ba mór mo míne.

Mé Líadan —
ro-carus-sa Cuirithir,
is fírinne ad-fíadar.

Gair bá-sa
i comaitecht Chuirithir,
fris-sium ba maith mo gnássa.

Céol caille
fom-chanad la Cuirithir
la fogur fairrge flainne.

Do-ménainn
ní cráidfed frimm Cuirithir
do dálaib cacha dénainn.

Ní chela:
ba hé-sium mo chrideserc
cía no carainn cách cena.

Joyfully
but that God had come between us then
had I granted what he begged of me.

Not unwise
is the way that he is taking now,
enduring pain and gaining Paradise.

Great folly
where once I showed such gentleness
to set Cuirithir against me!

Líadan I;
they say that I loved Cuirithir,
nor would I, if I could, deny.

The while I bless
that I was in his company
and was treating him with tenderness.

A woodland breeze
was my melody with Cuirithir
sounding harmony of reddening seas.

It seemed thus:
the last thing I would ever do
was a deed to come between us.

Cry clearly:
if any lovers this heart cherishes,
he its darling, loved most dearly.

Deilm ndega
ro-tethainn mo chride-se,
ro-fess nícon bía cena.


# XIV

## Cride Hé

Cride hé,
    daire cnó,
ócán é,
    pócán dó.


# XV

## Aithbe Dam Cen Bés Moro

Aithbe dam cen bés moro —
    sentu fom-dera croan;
toirse oca cía dono? —
    sona do-táet a loan.

Is mé caillech Bérri Buí,
no-meilinn léini mbithnuí;
indíu táthum do séimi
ná melainn cid aithléini.

28

A cry of pain
and the heart within was rent in two,
without him never beats again.


# XIV

## Tender Lad

Tender lad,
　　　　a darling this,
grove of nuts,
　　　　　worth a kiss.


# XV

## Ebbing

The ebbing that has come on me
is not the ebbing of the sea.
What knows the sea of grief or pain? —
Happy tide will flood again.

I am the hag of Buí and Beare —
the richest cloth I used to wear.
Now with meanness and with thrift
I even lack a change of shift.

It moíni
cartar lib, nídat doíni;
sinni, indbaid marsaimme
batar doíni carsaimme.

Batar inmaini doíni
    ata maige mad-ríadam;
ba maith no-meilmis leo,
    ba becc no-mmoítis íaram.

Indíu trá cáin timgarat
    ocus ní mór nond-oídet;
cíasu becc do-n-indnagat
    is mór a mét no-mmoídet.

Carpait lúaith
ocus eich no beirtis búaid,
ro boí, denus, tuile díb;
bennacht ar ríg do-da-úaid.

Tocair mo chorp co n-aichri
    dochum adba dían aithgni;
tan bas mithig la mac nDé
    do-té do brith a aithni.

Ó do-éctar mo láma
    ot é cnámacha cáela,
nítat fíu turcbáil, taccu,
    súas tar na maccu cáema.

It is wealth
and not men that you love.
In the time that we lived
it was men that we loved.

Those whom we loved, the plains
we ride today bear their names;
gaily they feasted with laughter
nor boasted thereafter.

To-day they gather in the tax
but, come to handing out, are lax;
the very little they bestow
be sure that everyone will know.

Chariots there were, and we
had horses bred for victory.
Such things came in a great wave;
pray for the dead kings who gave.

Bitterly does my body race
seeking its destined place;
now let God's Son come and take
that which he gave of his grace.

These arms, these scrawny things you see,
        scarce merit now their little joy
when lifted up in blessing
        over sweet student boy.

Ot é cnámacha cáela
    ó do-éctar mo láma,
ba inmainiu tan gnítis
    bítis im ríga rána.

It fáilti na ingena
    ó thic dóib co Beltaine;
is deithbiriu dam-sa brón,
    sech am tróg, am sentainne.

Ní feraim cobrai milis,
    ní marbtar muilt dom banais;
is becc, is líath mo thrilis,
    ní líach droch-caille tarais.

Ní olc lium
ce beith caille finn form chiunn;
boí móirmeither cech datha
form chiunn oc ól dag-latha.

Ním-gaib format fri nach sen
inge nammá fri Feimen:
meisse, rom-melt forbaid sin,
buide beus barr Feimin.

Lia na Ríg hi Femun,
Caithir Rónáin hi mBregun,
cían ó ro-s-siachtat sína,
a lleicne nít sen-chrína.

These arms you see,
    these bony scrawny things,
had once more loving craft
    embracing kings.

When Maytime comes
    the girls out there are glad,
and I, old hag, old bones,
    alone am sad.

No wedding wether killed for me,
an end to all coquetry;
a pitiful veil I wear
on thin and faded hair.

Well do I wear
plain veil on faded hair;
many colours I wore
and we feasting before.

Were it not for Feven's plain
    I'd envy nothing old;
I have a shroud of aged skin,
    Feven's crop is gold.

Ronan's city there in Bregon
    and in Feven the royal standing stone,
why are their cheeks not weathered,
    only mine alone?

Is labar tonn moro máir,
ros-gab in gaim cumgabáil;
fer maith, mac mogo in-díu
ní freiscim do chéilidiu.

Is éol dam a ndo-gniat,
    rait ocus do-raat;
curchasa Átha Alma,
    is úar ind adba hi faat.

Is mó láu
nád muir n-oíted imma-ráu;
testa már mblíadnae dom chruth,
dáig fo-rroimled mo chétluth.

Is mó dé
dam-sa in-díu, cibé de;
gaibthium étach cid fri gréin,
do-fil áes dam, at-gén féin.

Sam oíted i rrabamar
do-miult cona fagamur;
gaim aís báides cech nduine,
domm-ánaic a fochmuine.

Ro-miult m'oítid ar thuus
is buide lem ron-gleus;
cid becc mo léim dar duae
níbu nuae in bratt beus.

Winter comes and the sea will rise
    crying out with welcoming wave;
but no welcome for me from nobleman's son
    or from son of a slave.

What they do now, I know, I know:
    to and fro they row and race;
but they who once sailed Alma's ford
    rest in a cold place.

It's more than a day
    since I sailed youth's sea,
beauty's years not devoured
    and sap flowing free.

It's more than a day, God's truth,
that I'm lacking in youth;
I wrap myself up in the sun —
I know Old Age, I see him come.

There was a summer of youth
    nor was autumn the worst of the year,
but winter is doom
    and its first days are here.

God be thanked, I had joy of my youth.
    I swear that it's true,
if I hadn't leapt the wall
    this old cloak still were not new.

Is álainn in bratt úaine
    ro-scar mo Rí tar dromman;
is sáer in Fer no-d-lúaidi:
    do-rat loí fair íar lommad.

Aminecán morúar dam
    — cech n-érchaín is erchraide —
íar feis fri caindlib sorchaib
    bith i ndorchuib derthaige!

Rom-boí denus la ríga
oc ól meda ocus fína;
    indíu ibim medcuisce
eter sentainni crína.

Rop ed mo choirm: cóid in midc,
    ropo toil Dé cecham-theirp
oc do guidi-siu, a Dé bí,
    do-rat a chró clí fri feirg.

Ad-cíu form brott brodrad n-aís,
ro-gab mo chíall mo thogaís;
líath a finn ásas trim thoinn,
is samlaid crotball senchruinn.

Rucad úaim-se mo súil des
día reic ar thír mbithdíles;
ocus rucad int súil chlé
do formach a foirdílse.

The Lord on the world's broad back
    threw a lovely cloak of green;
first fleecy, then it's bare,
    and again the fleece is seen.

All beauty is doomed.
    God! Can it be right
to kneel in a dark prayer-house
    after feasting by candlelight?

I sat with kings drinking wine and mead
    for many a day,
and now, a crew of shrivelled hags,
    we toast in whey.

Be this my feast, these cups of whey;
    and let me always count as good
the vexing things that come of Christ
    who stayed God's ire with flesh and blood.

The mind is not so clear,
    there's mottling of age on my cloak,
grey hairs sprouting through skin,
    I am like a stricken oak.

For deposit on heaven
    of right eye bereft,
I concluded the purchase
    with loss of the left.

Tonn tuili
        ocus ind í aithbi áin,
a ndo-beir tonn tuili dait
        beirid tonn aithbi as do láim.

Tonn tuili
        ocus ind aile aithbi,
dom-áncatar-sa uili
        conda éola a n-aithgni.

Tonn tuili
ní cos tar socht mo chuili;
        cid mór mo dám fo deimi
fo-cress lám forru uili.

Mad ro-feissed mac Maire
        co mbeith fo chlí mo chuile:
cení dernus gart cenae
        ní érburt 'nac' fri duine.

Tróg n-uile! —
        doíriu dúilib don duiniu
nád ndecha asind aithbiu-se
        feib do-ndecha asin tuiliu.

Mo thuile,
        is maith con-roíter m'aithne;
ra-sóer Ísu mac Maire
        conda toirsech co aithbe.

Great wave of flood
   and wave of ebb and lack!
What flooding tide brings in
      the ebbing tide takes back.

Great wave of flood
      and wave of ebbing sea,
the two of them I know
      for both have washed on me.

Great wave of flood
      brings no step to silent cellar floor;
a hand fell on all the company
      that feasted there before.

The Son of Mary knew right well
      he'd walk that floor one day;
grasping I was, but never sent
      man hungry on his way.

Pity Man! —
      If only like the elements he could
come out of ebbing in the very way
      that he comes out of flood.

Christ left with me on loan
      flood tide of youth, and now it seems
there's ebb and misery, for Mary's Son
      too soon redeems.

Céin mair ailén mora máir,
dosn-ic tuile íarna tráig;
os mé, ní frescu dom-í
tuile tar éisi n-aithbi.


# XVI

## Fégaid Úaib

Fégaid úaib
sair fo thúaid
in muir múaid
    mílach;
adba rón
rebach, rán,
ro-gab lán
    línad.


# XVII

## Ná Luig, Ná Luig

Ná luig, ná luig
    fót fora taí:
gairit bía fair,
    fota bía faí.

Blessed the island in the great sea
    with happy ebb and happy flood.
For me, for me alone, no hope:
    the ebbing is for good.


# XVI

## The Sea

Look you out
northeastwards
over mighty ocean,
    teeming with sea-life;
home of seals,
sporting, splendid,
its tide has reached
    fullness.


# XVII

## The World

Take no oath, take no oath
    by the sod you stand upon:
you walk it short while
    but your burial is long.

Ná len, ná len
    in domun cé,
ná car, ná car,
    sel bec a ré.

Ná sir, ná sir
    in saegul seng,
ná gab, ná gab,
    ná tuit 'na chenn.

Baí sunn indé,
    ba gel a gné,
ní fil indiu
    acht 'na chrú fó chré.

Atá 'na rith
    mar théit in muir,
teich úaid i céin,
    ná héir, ná luig.


# XVIII

## M'áenurán Dam Isa Slíab

M'áenurán dam isa slíab,
    a rí grían rob soraid sét;
ním nessa éc ina meing
    indás no beinn tríchait chét.

42

Pay no heed, pay no heed
        to the world and its way,
give no love, give no love
        to what lasts but a day.

Have no care, have no care
        for the meaningless earth,
lay not hold, lay not hold
        on its gaiety and mirth.

A man fair of face
        was here yesterday;
now he is nothing
        but blood beneath clay.

The world is running out
        like the ebbing sea:
fly far from it
        and seek safety.


# XVIII

## Fate

I walk the lonely mountain road —
my King of Suns — and darkest glen,
no nearer death, though I be alone,
than fared I with three thousand men.

Cía no beinn-sea tríchait chét
    dind ócbaid tét, tenna a cnis,
dia tí caingen in báis brais
    ní fil daingen gabas fris.


Ní fil inill i nach dú
do mac duini acht rob trú;
ní cúala nech díambad toich
    belach fors ngondais étroich.


Cía dúthraigid nech mo brath,
cid santach imm scribulrath,
nó corob dén fíadat finn,
cía im-ráidi, ní cumaing.


Ní cumaing duinén in-díu
mo sáegul do thimdibiu,
acht in rí ro-delb in sam,
coimmdiu nime ocus talman.


Ním derban do thecht for fecht
cía sréidid nech i n-airecht;
fót for ro-delbad mo lecht,
isam écen a thairecht,


Ním derban d'imthecht m'áenur,
    sáegul rom delba, ním roisc;
ní tíag don biuth corba trú,
    ní tuit in cnú corba foisc.

Though fared I forth three thousand strong,
all lusty lads with bodies tough,
and mighty death came stalking me,
would they ward him off, were they enough?

If one be fey there's no safe place
and seeking sanctuary is vain,
while seems to me scarce natural
a path whereon the undoomed are slain.

A man may think to take my life,
appropriate my purse and pence,
but till the fair Lord gives assent
he'll plot and plan, and I'll not hence.

Where today stands any man
with power to snatch my life away?
None but the Maker of earth and sky,
the Shaper of the Summer-day.

Signs do not stop me setting out
— Did someone sneeze? — for my last breath
will be when foot compulsively
treads the awaiting sod of death.

I fear no more to walk alone;
let world which shaped me, gave me birth,
take not untimely back but wait
for nut-ripe falling to the earth.

In láech renas a chneas mbán
    isind áth fri galus ngúr,
ní nessa dó éc, cid báeth,
    indás don gáeth bís ar cúl.

Cía dú do fiur chonaire
    cuingid comairge for sét?
Isin chomairgi do-thét
    cate a chomairge ar éc?

Aminecán! Cía dono
do neuch imgabáil gono;
tairic a laithe báeguil
do chách i ciunn a sáeguil

For fáesam Dé uasail áin,
    athair noí ngrád spirut nóeb,
ním reilce i n-úathaib báis báin
    nó i ngráin cía dom-ecma im óen.

# XIX

## Flamina Nos Boreae
### SEDULIUS SCOTTUS

Flamina nos Boreae miro canentia vultu
    Perterrent subitis motibus atque minis:
Tellus ipsa tremit nimio perculsa pavore,
    Murmurat et pelagus duraque saxa gemunt,

The lad who risks his shining skin
in that ford yonder opposing might,
must he, then, be nearer death
than the skulker from the fight?

And why this seeking company?
Is it, perhaps, that you
are set on scaring death away
in awe of a great retinue?

Indeed, indeed, avoiding death
takes too much time and too much care,
and then, at the end of all,
he catches each one unaware.

May nine ranks of angels and my God
be ever watchful over me,
from terror, from caverns of white death
protecting, bearing company.


# XIX

## The Arrival at Liège
### SEDULIUS SCOTTUS

Dread-visaged Boreas blows rimy blasts and we
shrink back in terror from sudden darts and threats;
trembling the land, white-stricken with great fear,
and sea cries out and the hard rocks moan;

Aereos tractus Aquilo nunc vastat iniquus
Vocibus horrisonis murmuribusque tonans,
Lactea nubifero densantur vellera caelo,
Velatur nivea marcida terra stola,
Labuntur subito silvoso vertice crines
Nec stat harundineo robur et omne modo,
Titan, clarifico qui resplendebat amictu,
Abscondit radios nunc faciemque suam.
Nos tumidus Boreas vastat — miserabile visu —
Doctos grammaticos presbiterosque pios:
Namque volansAquilo non ulli parcit honori
Crudeli rostro nos laniando suo. —

Fessis ergo favens, Hartgari floride praesul,
Sophos Scottigenas suscipe corde pio:
Scandere sic valeas caelestia templa beatus,
Aetheream Solimam perpetuamque Sion.

Praesulis eximii clementia mensque serena
Flamina devicit rite superba domans.
Suscepit blandus fessosque loquacibus austris
Eripuit ternos dapsilitate sophas;
Et nos vestivit, triplici ditavit honore
Et fecit proprias pastor amoenus oves.

now he menaces the spaces of the air
with dread-arousing cries and thundering roar;
sky's milky fleece is covered with glowering cloud
and earth stands pallid in a snow-white gown;
and suddenly the woodland sheds its hair,
stout oak starts shaking like a reed;
the sun, that once had shone resplendently,
withholds his rays, now wholly hides his face;
ah woe! tumultuous Boreas has us all undone,
we learned teachers, yes, and pious priests,
for eagle Northwind has no regard of state
and mangles even us with cruel beak.

Then, Hartgar, powerful prelate, raise the weak,
cherish the learned Irish with gentle heart,
so, blessed, in heaven's high temples may you walk,
celestial Jerusalem and enduring Zion.

Great prelate! His mercy and his quiet mind
conquered the blasts and tamed old Boreas' pride;
kindly he led the weary in, and bountiful
snatched three scholars from the howling winds,
clothing us and honouring all three
so we became that gentle shepherd's sheep.

# XX

## Vestri Tecta Nitent Luce Serena

Vestri tecta nitent luce serena;
Florent arte nova culmina picta;
Rident atque tolo multicolora
Et formosa micant scemata plura.
Non sic, Hesperidum hortule, flores,
Marcescis subitis qui cito dampnis:
Nam vestrae violae seu rosa pulchra
Inhaesere tolis perpete sede;
Sic ostrum rubeum, sic iacincthus
Non horrent tumidi flamina Nothi.

Nostri tecta nigrant perpete nocte;
Intus nulla nitet gratia lucis;
Pictae vestis abest pulchra venustas;
Clavis nulla regit ac sera nulla;
Absis nonque micat compta tabellis —
Sed fuligo tolo haeret in alto;
Si, Neptune, pluas imbribus atris,
Crebras rore gravi domata nostra;
Eurus si reboet murmure saevo,
Haec quassata tremit aula vetusta.

Caci talis erat mansio tetra;
Talis caecus erat iam Laborintus,
Instar qui fuerat noctis opacae.
Sic et nostra domus — heu nefas ingens —
Horret palliolo fuscida nigro:

# XX

## Hartgar's Palace
SEDULIUS SCOTTUS

Your halls are gleaming with a light serene
and latest style in art adorns the scene
with beauteous forms to populate your home
and many merry colours in your dome;
a garden of Hesperides each room
with flowers dancing in perpetual bloom,
the rose, the violets that never die
but cling to wall and cupola on high:
the withering southern blast may blow and blow
and purple, red or jacinth never know.

It's different where *we* live: perpetual night
within the house and ne'er a gleam of light;
no florid beauty decorates the walls,
no key nor bar protects us in our halls;
arches lack paint and scenic gaiety but
the ceiling has a pattern of soot.
Ah! Neptune, when you send us those dark showers
a heavy dew invades this house of ours;
be quiet, East Wind, nor raise your voice at all
or else the walls near tumble on us all.

A loathsome cave had Cacus, Vulcan's boy,
a labyrinth devoid of light and joy,
night's very image, full of dark and fear;
to put in brief — Ah, woe! — 'twas just like here.

Nam lucente die noctis imago
Crassescit vetulis aedibus istis.
Non haec apta domus, crede, sophistis,
Qui splendentis amant munera lucis —
Sed haec apta domus nicticoraci
Talparumque gregi mansio digna.
O Lantberte, nigros collige caecos
Omnes, oro, tuos transfer in istam:
Caecorum valeat semper in aevum
Haec obscura domus rite vocari.

Sed nunc, celse pater splendide pastor,
His succurre malis, o decus almum;
Dic verboque pio, quo decoretur
Haec umbrosa domus priva dierum:
Sit pulchrum laquear stigmate pictum;
Sit clavisque recens ac sera firma;
Mox glaucae, vitreae sintque fenestrae,
Quo Phebus radios dirigat almus
Perlustretque sophos crine decoro,
Praesul clare, tuos lucis amantes.

# XXI

## Nunc Viridant Segetes

Nunc viridant segetes, nunc florent germine campi,
Nunc turgent vites, est nunc pulcherrimus annus,
Nunc pictae volucres permulcent aethera cantu,
Nunc mare, nunc tellus, nunc caeli sidera rident.

Our dwelling shudders in a cloak of black.
When daylight comes she promptly sends it back,
grows ever blacker and assumes a guise
not fit, I say, for scholars or the wise,
such as love splendour and the gifts of light,
but more for moles and owls and things of night.
Oh, Hartgar! All such that cannot see
gather together and bring them here to me —
for this dark house a fitting use we'll find.
We'll christen it: 'Asylum for the Blind.'

Or else, great father, pastor with power and might,
come to our aid and set these matters right,
speaking the gracious word that workmen may
start on the job, let in the light of day;
first figures on ceiling paint, and we
have need of bar and bolt, have need of key;
then windows gleaming bright with sparkling glass
in such a way that rays of light may pass
shining for scholars, and warming hearts that do
but love, my lord, the light and sun and you.

# XXI

## Request For Meat And Drink
### SEDULIUS SCOTTUS

The crops are green and fields are all in flower,
budding the vine — the year now has its hour;
gay-painted songbirds fill the air with glee,
there's smile on land and sky and laughs the sea.

Ast nos tristificis perturbat potio sucis,
Cum medus atque Ceres, cum Bachi munera desint;
Heu — quam multiplicis defit substantia carnis,
Quam mitis tellus generat, quam roscidus aether.

Scriptor sum (fateor), sum Musicus alter et Orpheus,
Sum bos triturans, prospera quaeque volo,
Sum vester miles sophiae praeditus armis:
Pro nobis nostrum, Musa, rogato patrem.


# XXII

## De Strage Normannorum

Gaudeant caeli, mare, cuncta terra,
Gaudeat Christi populusque vernans;
Facta miretur domini tonantis
    Fortia patris.

Laudibus dignus bonitatis auctor,
Magnus in magnis opifex beatus,
Cuncta dispensat dominante nutu
    Sceptriger orbis.

Spes, salus mundi, pius ipse rector
Conterens pravos humiles coronat,
Sublevat valles reprimitque montes
    Celsa potestas.

Of mirth-provoking sap I too have need,
some beer, or Bacchus' gift, or perhaps some mead;
and then there's meat, produce of earth and sky,
and I have none, but ask the reason why.

Now, Muse, I write and sing, am Orpheus reborn,
but too have needs, the ox that treads the corn;
your champion I, with wisdom's arms I fight:
Off to the bishop, and tell him of my plight.


# XXII

## Defeat Of The Northmen
### SEDULIUS SCOTTUS

Rejoice you heavens, sea and all the land;
you people too who flower in Christ,
see the great deeds of the Lord, the Father,
    thundering Godhead.

Most worthy of praises, sole author of good,
great in great deeds, blessed creator,
holding firmament's sceptre and with nod of the brow
    all things disposing.

World's holy ruler, its hope and salvation,
levelling mountain, raising the valley,
crushing the wicked, crowning the humble,
    omnipotent power.

Qui facit rectis radiare verum
Lumen in cordis speculoque mentis,
Quos tegit semper pietate pollens
    Conditor almus.

Pauperes, dites, laici, potentes,
O coronate clericalis ordo,
Omnis aetatis decus atque sexus,
    Plaudite cuncti.

Brachium patris validum potentis
Ecce protrivit subita rebellem
Strage Normannum pietatis hostem:
    Gloria patri.

Proelium campo struitur patenti,
Splendor armorum radiat per auras,
Voce bellantum varia tremescit
    Machina caeli.

Tela sparserunt geminae phalanges,
Danus infelix sua dampna quaerit,
Ferreos imbres serit atque fixit
    Agmen inorme.

Quem sitiverunt varios per annos
Sanguinem sumunt rabidi tyranni:
Dulce fit cunctis satiare pectus
    Caede virorum.

Christ the true Light He causes to shine
on faithful hearts, on mirror of the mind,
cherishing them with constancy,
     sustaining creator.

You rich and poor, you high and humble,
clerics too, His tonsured order,
young and old, mankind and women,
     praise Him you all.

The stout strong arm of a powerful father
with sudden fury has now prostrated
foes of the faithful, the rebel Northman;
     glory to the Father.

The fight is joined on open plain
and weapons glitter in the limpid air
and warrior cry might seem to shake
     the scaffolding of sky.

Opposing lines unleash their spearshafts,
unhappy Northman counts his losses,
a mighty army aims and places
     its showers of iron.

Those who have thirsted down through the years
are quaffing the blood of a savage oppressor
and finding sweet savour in nourishing heart
     on the slaughter of men.

Quique foderunt foveas, ruere;
Quae fuit turris nimium superba,
Ecce curvatur nihilata Christo
        Gens inimica.

Sternitur grandis populusque fortis,
Tota contrita est maledicta massa,
Sorbet os mortis sobolem malignam:
        Laus tibi, Christe.

Hinc ferunt stragem populi fuisse:
Praeter ignotos hominesque vilis
Horrido campo nimio cruore
        Tres myriades.

Justus est iudex dominator orbis,
Christianorum decus omne Christus,
Gloriae princeps, domitor malorum
        Regmine summo.

Fortis est turris, clipeus salutis
Conterens bello validos gigantes,
Cuius excelsum super omne nomen
        Est benedictum.

Ultor existit populi fidelis,
Qui maris quondam tumidis procellis
Pressit Aegyptum, celeres rotasque
        Obruit imo.

Those who set snares stand there ensnared,
topples a tower reaching to the sky;
a hostile horde, swelling with pride,
    Christ has undone them.

There is there laid low a stout strong people,
a cursed mass has now been crumbled,
an evil issue death's maw has swallowed;
    be praised, O Christ.

Now can be reckoned a mighty slaughter:
count not unknown, count not the menials,
on that dread field lay bloody there
    three times ten thousand.

The judge is just, lord of the world,
Christ the true glory of Christian people,
magnificent ruler, vanquishing evil
    in high jurisdiction.

Great tower is He, and shield of salvation
undoing in battle the strength of the giants,
Whose name is high above all names
    and ever blessed.

A faithful people has that great avenger
who unleashed the sea in swelling torrents
on proud Egyptian, overwhelming all,
    chariots, horsemen.

Ostriger Jesus super omne regnat,
Quicquid excelsus genitor creavit,
Stirpe Davidis benedicta proles,
  Gloria nostra.

Cui rependatur tymiama voti,
Quem celebremus pietatis actu,
Cui melos promat super astra regi
  Fistula laudis.

Gloriae plausus, modulans osanna
Personet patrem genitumque Christum,
Spiritum sanctum: polus unda tellus,
  Glorificate.


# XXIII
## Justus Quid Meruit

Justus quid meruit, simplex, sine fraude maligna?
  Munera nec Bachi, non siceramque bibit,
Non hunc ebrietas deflexit tramite recti,
  Non epulae regum nec procerumque dapes:
Illi pastus erat sollemnicus herba per agros
  Ac dulcem potum limphida Mosa dabat:
Non ostri vestes rubei cupiebat avarus,
  Sed contentus erat pellicia tunica;
Nonque superbus equo lustrabat amoena virecta
  Sed propriis pedibus rite migrabat iter;
Non mendosus erat nec inania verba loquutus:
  Báá seu béé mystica verba dabat.

Christ wearing purple now reigns over
what high Begetter first created,
blessed scion of the House of David
    and our glory.

He to Whom we offer incense,
Whom we name in act of prayer,
King of stars Whom we intone
    on pipe of praise.

Now cry you glory and cry Hosanna,
now sing of Father, Christ begotten,
and Holy Spirit; sky, earth and water
    praise Him you all.


# XXIII

## On The Slaying of a Ram

### SEDULIUS SCOTTUS

Wherein his guilt — so simple, straight and true?
Bacchus he shunned, sherbet avoided too;
not him did liquor from narrow path entice,
not meal with king, or lesser lord, his vice;
his solemn feast was grazing on the grass,
his sweetest drink from brink of limpid Maas,
nor did he plead that he be vested in
purple or red — felt happy with a skin;
and never did he ride astride a horse
but steady on his legs he plied a course,
lied not, nor idle word did ever say,
but utterance of depth — just 'baa' and 'beh'.

Tu, bone multo, vale, nivei gregis inclite ductor,
  Heu quia nec vivum te meus hortus habet.
Forsan, amice, tibi fieret calidumque lavacrum —
  Non alia causa, iure sed hospitii;
Ipse ministrassem devoto pectore limphas
  Cornigero capita, calcibus atque tuis.
Te (fateor) cupii; viduam matremque cupisco,
  Fratres atque tuos semper amabo. Vale.


# XXIV

## Aut Lego Vel Scribo

Aut lego vel scribo, doceo scrutorve sophiam:
  Obsecro celsithronum nocte dieque meum.
Vescor, poto libens, rithmizans invoco Musas,
  Dormisco stertens: oro deum vigilans.
Conscia mens scelerum deflet peccamina vitae:
  Parcite vos misero, Christe Maria, viro.


# XXV

## In India

Ro- fess a maith as cech aird,
a magnéit, a hadamaint,
is a margréit a hur i n-or,
a hór is a carrmocol.

Adieu good chief of gleaming herd — alas!
   I see you not a-feeding on my grass.
   Ah! Were you there a hot bath I had planned
   (only to please the guest you understand!)
   and self would minister with devoted breast
   to head and horn and hoof and all the rest.
   You have I loved, and love your widow too,
   mother I love, and brothers all — Adieu.

# XXIV

## Confession
### SEDULIUS SCOTTUS

I read and write and teach, philosophy peruse.
I eat and freely drink, with rhymes invoke the muse,
I call on heaven's throne both night and day,
snoring I sleep, or stay awake and pray.
And sin and fault inform each act I plan:
Ah! Christ and Mary, pity this miserable man.

# XXV

## India
### AIRBERTACH MAC COISSE

Its goods are known far and wide,
its lodestone, its adamant,
from land to land its pearls,
its gold and its carbuncle.

A hóenbennach for cóe gnáith,
a ggáeth féthamail fírbláith,
a heliphaint co mbríg bil,
a búain fo dí in cach bliadain.


# XXVI
## Ísucán

Ísucán
    alar lemm im dísiurtán;
cía beth cléirech co lín sét
    is bréc uile acht Ísucán.


Altram alar lemm im thig
    ní altram nach dóerathaig;
Ísu co feraib nime
    frim chride cech n-óenadaig.


Ísucán óc mo bithmaith,
    ernaid ocus ní maithmech;
in rí con-ic na uili
    cen a guidi bid aithrech.


Ísu úasal ainglide,
    noco cléirech dergnaide;
alar lemm im dísiurtán
    Ísu mac na Ebraide.

Its unicorn on wonted path,
smooth and truly gentle breeze,
elephants with vicious power,
harvest twice in every year.

# XXVI

## St. Ite's Song

Ísucán,
I nurse him in my lonely place;
though a priest have stores of wealth,
all is vain save Ísucán.

The nursling fostered in my house
is no son of base-born churl;
Jesus comes with heavenly host
to my breast each even-tide.

Young Ísucán, my eternal good,
bestows, is not witholding;
woe to him who does not pray
the king with power in everything.

Jesus, noble, angel-like,
not a common priest is he;
I nurse, here in my lonely place,
Jesus, son of Jewish maiden.

Maic na ruirech, maic na ríg,
    im thír cía do-ísatán,
ní úaidib saílim sochur,
    is tochu lemm Ísucán.

Canaid cóir, a ingena,
    d'fiur dliges bar císucán;
atá 'na phurt túasucán
    cía beith im ucht Ísucán.


## XXVII

## Atá Uarboth Dam I Caill

Atá úarboth dam i caill,
    nís-fitir acht mo Fhíada:
uinnius di-síu, coll an-all,
    bile rátha nosn-íada.

Dí ersainn fraích fri fulong
    ocus fordorus féithe;
feraid in chaill imma cress
    a mess for mucca méithe.

Mét mo boithe: beccnat becc,
    baile sétae sognath;
canaid sian mbinn día beinn
    ben a lleinn co londath.

        *       *       *

Sons of kings, both great and small,
may come this way to visit me;
but my profit is not in them,
I rather choose Ísucán.

Chant a choir-song, virgins
for him to whom your rent is due;
in his dwelling high above
and at my breast is Ísucán.


# XXVII

## The Hermit

I have a bothy in the wood —
none knows it but the Lord, my God;
one wall an ash, the other hazel,
and a great fern makes the door.

The doorsteps are of heather,
the lintel of honeysuckle;
and wild forest all around
drops mast for well-fed swine.

This size my hut: the smallest thing,
homestead amid well-trod paths;
a woman — blackbird clothed and coloured —
is singing sweetly from its gable.

*       *       *

Monga lebra ibair éoglais,
    nósta cél!
Caín in magan márglas darach
    darsin sén.

Aball ubull (már a ratha)
    mbruidnech mbras;
barr dess dornach, collán cnobecc
    cróebach nglas.

Glére thibrat, essa uisci,
    úais do dig;
bruinnit ilair, cáera ibair,
    fidait fir.

Foilgit impe mucca cenntai,
    cadlaid, uirc,
mucca alltai, oiss aird, eillti,
    bruicnech, bruic.

Buidnech, sídech, slúag tromm tírech,
    dál dom thig;
ina erchaill tecat cremthainn,
    álainn sin.

*     *     *

Líne ugae, mil, mess, melle,
    Dia dod-roíd;
ubla milsi, mónainn derca,
    dercna froích.

*     *     *

Smooth the tresses of yew-green yew-trees,
     glorious portent;
place delicious with great green oakwoods
     increasing blessing.

Tree of apples huge and magic,
     great its graces;
crop in fistfulls from clustered hazel,
     green and branching.

Sparkling wells and water-torrents,
     best for drinking;
green privet there and bird-cherry
     and yew-berries.

Resting there are herded swine,
     goats and piglings;
wild swine too, deer and doe,
     speckled badgers.

Great woodland bands troop like fairies
     to my bothy;
and great delight when timid foxes
     show their faces.

                    *         *         *

Eggs in clutches and God gives mast,
     honey, heath-pease;
sweet the apples and the berries
     of bog and heather.

                    *         *         *

Cúach meda colláin chunnla
co ndáil daith;
durcháin donna, dristin monga
mérthain maith.

Mad fri samrad suairc snobrat
somlas mlas,
curair, orcáin, foltáin glaise,
glaine glas.

Céola ferán mbruinne forglan
foram ndil,
dordán smálcha caíne gnáthcha
úas mo thig.

Tellinn, cíarainn, cerdán cruinne,
crónán séim;
gigrainn, cadain, gair ré Samain
seinm ngairb chéir.

\* \* \*

Tecat caínfinn, corra, faílinn,
fos-cain cúan;
ní céol ndogra cerca odra
a fráech rúad.

\* \* \*

Fogur gaíthe fri fid flescach
forglas néol,
essa aba, esnad eala,
álainn céol.

A cup of mead from noble hazel,
    swift the service;
acorns brown, bramble tresses
    and their berries.

Then in summer pleasant mantle
    of tasty savour;
marjoram, earth-nuts, and the tresses
    of the streamlet.

Pigeons cooing, breasts are gleaming,
    beloved flutter;
on my house-top constant music,
    song of thrushes.

Bees and chafers, gentle humming
    and soft crooning;
wild geese come with rough dark music
    before All Hallows.

*       *       *

Then come dear white ones, herons, sea-gulls
    sea-chant hearing;
no harsh music when grouse is calling
    from russet heather.

*       *       *

The sound of wind in branching trees,
    day grey and cloudy;
stream in torrent, swans are singing,
    sweet the music.

71

Caíne ailmi ardom-peitet,
    ní íarna creic,
do Chríst cech than ní messa dam
    oldás deit.


Cid maith lat-su a ndo-mil-siu,
    mó cach maín,
buidech lem-sa do-berr dam-sa
    óm Chríst chaín.


Cen úair n-augrai, cen deilm ndebtha
    immut foich,
buidech dond Fhlaith do-beir cach maith
    dom im boith.


# XXVIII

## Mé Éba

Mé Éba, ben Ádaim uill;
    mé ro-sáraig Ísu thall,
mé ro-thall nem ar mo chloinn,
    cóir is mé do-chóid 'sa crann.


Ropa lem rítheg dom réir,
    olc in míthoga rom-thár,
olc in cosc cinad rom-chrín,
    for-ír! ní hidan mo lám.

I hear the soughing of the pine-trees
   and pay no money;
I am richer far through Christ, my Lord,
   than ever you were.

Though you enjoy all you consume
   and wealth exceeding,
I am grateful for the riches
   my dear Christ brings me.

No hour of trouble like you endure,
   no din of combat:
I thank the Prince who so endows me
   in my bothy.


# XXVIII

## Eve

I am Eve, great Adam's wife,
because of me has Jesus died;
it were I, thief of my children's heaven
by all rights were crucified.

I had a king's house to my wish,
but made an evil choice one day
that withered both my flesh and soul
and left my hand unclean this way.

Mé tuc in n-uball an-úas,
    do-chúaid tar cumang mo chraís;
in céin marat-sam re lá
    de ní scarat mná re baís.


Ní bíad eigred in cach dú,
    ní bíad geimred gáethmar glé,
ní bíad iffern, ní bíad brón,
    ní bíad óman minbad mé.


# XXIX
## A Chrínóc, Cubaid Do Cheól
MAEL ÍSU Ó BROLCHÁIN

A Chrínóc, cubaid do cheól,
    cenco bat fíróc at fíal;
ro-mósam túaid i tír Néill
    tan do-rónsam feis réid ríam.

Rop hí m'áes tan ro-foís lem,
    a bé níata in gáesa grinn,
daltán clíabglan cáem nád camm,
    maccán mall secht mbliadan mbinn.

Bámar for bith Banba bailc
    cen éilniud anma ná cuirp,
mo lí lasrach lán dot seirc
    amail geilt cen aslach uilc.

74

Unclean! It snatched forbidden fruit
compulsively — it must, it must;
and hence forever, while women be,
live passion, folly, greed and lust.

There were no ice in any place,
there were no winter, no stormy sea,
there were no hell and no regrets,
there were no terror but for me.


# XXIX

## To An Old Psalm-book
MÁEL ÍSU Ó BROLCHÁIN

Crínóc, lady of measured melody,
    not young, but with modest maiden mind,
together once in Niall's northern land
    we slept, we two, as man and womankind.

You came and slept with me for that first time,
    (skilled wise amazon annihilating fears)
and I a fresh-faced boy, not bent as now,
    a gentle lad of seven melodious years.

There we were then on that firm Irish earth
    desirous, but in pure and mystic sense;
burning with love my flesh, still free from fault
    as fool of God in smitten innocence.

Erlam do chomairle chóir,
    dóig nos-togamne in cech tír
is ferr rográd dot gaeis géir,
    ar comrád réid frisin Ríg.


Ro-foís la cethrar íar sin
    im díaid cen nach methlad mer;
ro-fetar, is beóda in blad,
at glan cen pheccad fri fer.


Fo deóid dom rúachtais do-rís
    íar cúartaib scís, gleó co ngaeis;
do-dechaid temel tart gnúis,
    cen drúis is dered dot aeis.


At inmain lem-sa cen locht,
    rot-bía mo chen-sa cen cacht;
ní léicfe ar mbádud i péin,
    fo-gabam crábud léir lat.


Lán dot labrad in bith búan,
    adbal do rith tar cach rían;
día seichmis cech día do dán
    ro-seismis slán co Día ndían.


Do-beire do thimna in toí
    do chách co himda ar bith ché;
síthlai dúin uile in cech ló
    ní gó guide díchra Dé.

Your counsel is ever there to hand,
    we choose it, following you in everything;
love of your word is the best of loves,
    our gentle conversation with the King.

Guiltless you are of any sin with man,
    fair is your name, and bright, and without stain,
although I know that when you went from me
    each in his turn, four lay where I had lain.

And now you come, your final pilgrimage,
    wearied with toil and travel, grimed with dust,
wise still but body not immaculate:
    time it is that ravished you, not lust.

Again I offer you a faultless love,
    a love unfettered for which surely we
will not be punished in the depths of hell
    but together ever walk in piety.

Seeking the presence of elusive God
    wandering we stray, but the way is found,
following the mighty melodies that with you
    throughout the pathways of the world resound.

Not ever silent, you bring the word of God
    to all who in the present world abide,
and then through you, through finest mesh,
    Man's earnest prayer to God is purified.

Do-rata Día dellraid dúin
    a ré frit ar menmain mín
rop rolainn frinn gnúis Ríg réil
    íar n-ar léimm ór colainn chrín.


# XXX

## A Dhé, Tuc Dam Topur nDér

A Dhé, tuc dam topur ndér
    do díl mo chinad, ní chél;
ní toirthech talam cen bráen,
    ním náem cén anam cen dér.


# XXXI

## Mo Chinaid I Comláine
### MAEL ÍSU Ó BROLCHÁIN

Mo chinaid i comláine,
    in guth, in gním i cride,
rith mo rúathar rográinne
    dílig dam, a Dé nime.

In tan ropsa móethóclach
    ropsam dermatach dligid;
ba lainn lemm mo bóethphócad
    do mnáib détgelaib dilib.

78

May the King give us beauty back again
    who ever did his will with quiet mind,
may he look on us with eagerness and love,
    our old and perished bodies left behind.


# XXX

## Tears

God, give me a well of tears
    my sins to hide,
or I am left like arid earth
    unsanctified.


# XXXI

## Confession
MÁEL ÍSU Ó BROLCHÁIN

Forgiveness, God, for all my sins
    I seek at last,
the sin in word, the deed in heart,
    foul sin compassed.

In heedless youth I broke the rule,
    made grievous slips,
offered fair women of gleaming teeth
    lascivious lips.

Tan atám ar senórach,
    íar cech thuitim co trúaige,
ní ferr lemm lá fledóla
    iná déra dar mo grúaide.


# XXXII

## Teicht Do Róim

Teicht do Róim,
    mór saído, becc torbai!
In rí chon-daigi hi foss,
manim-bera latt, ní fogbai.


# XXXIII

## Is Mo Chen In Maiten Bán

Is mo chen in maiten bán,
do-thét ar lár m'airiuclán,
is mo chen don tí rus-foí,
in maiten buadach bithnaí.

A ingen Aidche úaille,
a siúr na Gréine glúaire,
is mo chen, a maiten bán,
foillsiges orm mo lebrán.

Now I am an old, old man
and after sinful years
I seek no feast but that my cheeks
be wet with tears.

# XXXII

## Pilgrimage To Rome

Pilgrim, take care your journey's not in vain,
a hazard without profit, without gain;
the King you seek you'll find in Rome, it's true,
but only if he travels on the way with you.

# XXXIII

## Dawn

Come into my dark oratory,
be welcome the bright morn,
and blessed He who sent you,
victorious, self-renewing dawn.

Maiden of good family.
Sun's sister, daughter of proud Night,
ever-welcome the fair morn
that brings my mass-book light.

It-chí agaid cach tige,
soillsigi túaith is fine,
is mo chen, a muingel mass,
acainn, a órchaín amnass.


# XXXIV

## Ach, A Luin

Ach, a luin, is buide duit
    cáit 'sa muine i fuil do net,
a díthrebaig nád clinn cloc,
    is binn boc síthamail t'fet.


# XXXV

## Robad Mellach, A Meic Mo Dé

Robad mellach, a meic mo Dé,
    dingnaib réimenn
ascnam tar tuinn topur ndílenn
    dochum nÉirenn.

Co mag nEólairg, sech Beinn Foibne,
    tar Loch Febail,
airm i cluinfinn cuibdius cubaid
    ac na helaib.

Touching the face of each house,
    illumining every kin,
white-necked and gold-bedecked —
    welcome, imperious one. Come in.


# XXXIV

## The Blackbird

Blackbird, it is well for you
wherever in the thicket be your nest,
hermit that sounds no bell,
sweet, soft, fairylike is your note.


# XXXV

## Colum Cille's Exile

This were pleasant, O Son of God,
    with wondrous coursing
to sail across the swelling torrent
    back to Ireland.

To Eólarg's plain, past Benevanagh,
    across Loch Feval,
and there to hear the swans in chorus
    chanting music.

Sluag na Feblán robtis faíltig
    rér séol súntach,
día rísed Port na Ferg faíltech
    in Derg Drúchtach.

Rom-lín múich i n-ingnais Éirenn
    díamsa coimsech,
'san tír aineóil conam-tharla
    taideóir toirsech.

Trúag in turus do-breth form-sa,
    a rí rúine,
Ach, níma ndechad bu-déine
    do chath Chúile!

Ba ma-ngénar do mac Dímma
    'na chill chredlaig,
airm i cluinfinn tíar i nDurmaig
    — mian dom menmain —

fúaim na gaíthe frisin leman
    ardon-peite,
golgaire in luin léith co n-aite
    íar mbéim eite.

Éistecht co moch i Ros Grencha
    frisin damraid,
coicetal na cúach don fidbaid
    ar brúach samraid.

And when my boat, the Derg Drúchtach,
    at last made harbour
in Port na Ferg the joyful Foyle-folk
    would sound a welcome.

I ever long for the land of Ireland
    where I had power,
an exile now in midst of strangers,
    sad and tearful.

Woe that journey forced upon me,
    O King of Secrets;
would to God I'd never gone there,
    to Cooldrevne.

Well it is for son of Dímma
    in his cloister,
and happy I but were I hearing
    with him in Durrow

the wind that ever plays us music
    in the elm-trees,
and sudden cry of startled blackbird,
    wing a-beating.

And listen early in Ros Grencha
    to stags a-belling,
and when cuckoo, at brink of summer,
    joins in chorus.

Ro grádaiges íatha Éirenn,
  deilm cen ellach;
feis re Comgall, cúairt co Caindech
  robad mellach.


# XXXVI

## Fil Súil nGlais

Fil súil nglais
fégbas Éirinn dar a hais;
nocho n-aicceba íarmo-thá
firu Érenn nách a mná.


# XXXVII

## Tadhbhás Do Lugh, Leannán Teamhra
### GOFRAIDH FIONN Ó DÁLAIGH

Tadhbhás do Lugh, leannán Teamhra,
  thoir i nEamhain,
dá ránaig sé ar súr gach domhain
  Múr Té, Teamhair.

Dúnta an chathair ar cionn Logha,
  laoch ro thoghsam;
téid gusan múr sleamhain slioschorr,
  beanaidh boschrann.

I have loved the land of Ireland
　　— I cry for parting;
to sleep at Comgall's, visit Canice,
　　this were pleasant.


# XXXVI

## The Backward Look

Grey eye there is
that backward looks and gazes;
never will it see again
Ireland's women, Ireland's men.


# XXXVII

## The Coming Of Lugh
GOFRAIDH FIONN Ó DÁLAIGH

East in Eamhain
Tara's lover, Lugh beheld
　　Té's fortress Tara
and leaving other lands he sought it.

He found the city closed before him,
　　our chosen hero;
against its portals, smooth and tapering
　　he strikes the hammer.

Ar an doirseóir ris an deaghlaoch
    fa doirbh ruaigfhearg:
'Cáit asa dtig an fear áith, ógard,
    bláith, geal, gruaiddearg.

Ris an doirseóir
adubhairt Lugh nár loc iomghuin:
'File meise a hEamhain Abhlaigh,
    ealaigh, iobhraigh.'

          *       *       *


Ar gcluinsin ar chan an macaomh,
    mór a thairm-séin,
d'agallaimh Thuath Dé don doirseóir,
    luath é ainnséin.

'Fear san doras', ar an doirseóir,
    'rén doirbh coimmeas,
an uile cheard ar a chommus,
    an dearg doinndeas'.

'Damadh é Lugh, leannán Fódla
    na bhfonn sriobhfhann
do bheith ann', ar Tuath Dé Danann,
    'dob é a ionam'.

'Geall n-éagaisg ón fhior san doras,
    damhna leisge,
nocho ndearnadh d'úir ná d'uisge
    dúil dán dleisde'.

88

Said the doorman to the hero,
    stout in combat:
'Whence comes the youth so tall and stalwart,
    smooth, bright, red-cheeked?'

To the doorman answered Lugh
    who feared no combat:
'A poet I from Appled Eamhain
    of swans and yew-trees.'

       \*     \*     \*

When he heard the youth's recital,
    great and famous,
haste he made to Danu's people
    with the message.

'A youth is coming,' said the doorman,
    'hard to match him.
All the arts are in his power,
    comely strong one.'

'Were it Lugh, the gentle-rivered
    Ireland's lover,
that were there,' said Danu's people,
    'it were timely.'

'To match in beauty him who stands there
    were cause for slowness,
no creature made of earth or water
    yet can dare it.'

'A thaobh, a aghaidh, a earla,
    eochair thogha,
triar ar snuadh aoil agus umha,
    agus fhola'.


'Binne a theanga
ná téada meannchrot 'gá míndeilbh,
    ón sádhail suan,
i lámhaibh suadh agá sírsheinm'.


'Issé sin', ar sluag na cathrach,
    'ar gceann báidhe,
    aonmhac Eithne,
saorshlat ar nach beirthe báire'.


'Brosdaighthear', ar Tuath Dé Danann,
    'doirseóir Teamhra,
d'ionnsoighidh na craoibhe cubhra,
    aoighe Eamhna'.


# XXXVIII

## Athesc Findabrach

Ba hed íarum athesc Findabrach,
nach álaind at-chíd:
ba háildiu lee
Fróech do acsin tar dublind,

'His face, his hair, his body,
    key of choosing,
like blood and bronze, and lime for whiteness
    is the triad.'


'His tongue is sweeter
than lute-strings finely fashioned
    for gentle sleep
and ever played by expert fingers.'


'It is he,'
said Tara's people, 'our goal of loving,
    Eithne's lone son,
noble scion never conquered.'


'Doorman of Tara, let you hasten,'
    said Danu's people,
'to receive the branch of fragrance,
    guest from Eamhain.'


# XXXVIII

## Findabair Remembers Fróech

This, thereafter, is what Findabair used to say,
seeing anything beautiful:
it would be more beautiful for her
to see Fróech crossing the dark water,

in corp do rogili,
ocus in folt do roáilli,
ind aiged do chumtachtai,
int šúil do roglaissi,
is é móethóclách
cen locht, cen ainim,
co n-agaid focháel, forlethain,
is é díriuch dianim,
in chráeb cosnaib cáeraib dergaib
eter in mbrágait ocus in n-aigid ngil.
Is ed at-bered Findabair:
nícon acca ní
ro-sáissed leth
nó trian do chruth.

# XXXIX

## Eterne Deus

Eterne Deus,
duo sunt in Momonia
qui destruunt nos et bona nostra,
videlicet comes Ermonie
et comes Dessemonie
cum eorum sequacibus,
quos in fine destruet Dominus
per Christum Dominum nostrum.
Amen.

body for shining whiteness,
hair for loveliness,
face for shapeliness,
eye for blue-greyness,
a well-born youth
without fault or blemish,
face broad above, narrow below,
and he straight and perfect,
the branch with its red berries
between throat and white face.
This is what Findabair used to say:
She had never seen
anything a half
or a third as beautiful as he.


# XXXIX

## The Earls Of Ormond And Desmond

Eternal God,
there are two in Munster
who destroy us and what is ours.
These are the Earl of Ormond
and the Earl of Desmond
with those who follow them,
whom in the end the Lord will destroy
through Christ, our Lord.
Amen.

# XL

## An Droighneán Donn

Síleann céad fear gur léo féin mé
  nuair ólaim lionn,
is téann a dhá dtrian síos díom ag cuimhne
  ar do chomhrádh liom;
sneachta séidhte 's é dá shíor-chur
  ar sliabh Uí Fhloinn,
's tá mo ghrádh-sa mar bhláth na n-áirne
  ar an droighnéan donn.


# XLI

## Lughaidh, Tadhg Agus Tórna
### FLAITHRÍ Ó MAOIL CHONAIRE

Lughaidh, Tadhg agus Tórna,
  ollaimh eólcha bhúr dtalaimh,
coin iad go n-iomad bhfeasa
  ag troid fán easair fhalaimh.

# XL

## The Blackthorn Bush

A hundred men think I am theirs
    when I drink wine;
but they go away when I start to think
    on your talk and mine.
Slieve O'Flynn is quiet, silent
    with snowdrift's hush,
and my love is like sloe-blossom
    on the blackthorn bush.

# XLI

## Irish Scholars
### FLAITHRÍ Ó MAOIL CHONAIRE

Lughaidh, Tadhg and Tórna,
    your country's well-schooled lot,
what learned hounds they are
    fighting for an empty pot!

# Notes to the Poems

An effort has been made to keep the following notes at a minimum, but at the same time sufficient references are generally given to enable the reader to follow the full textual history of any poem, other than modern folk-poetry. Where a poem has been edited and translated in Gerard Murphy's *Early Irish Lyrics* (EIL), reference has been made to that source rather than to any other. EIM refers to Murphy's *Early Irish Metrics* and *Bruchstücke* refers to Kuno Meyer's *Bruchstücke der älteren Lyrik Irlands*. Murphy's excellent work has been of inestimable value in the preparation of many of the texts in the present volume.

I. The Irish text of this poem was included in the ninth century *Vita Tripartita*. It also survived in a seventh century version translated into Latin by Muirchú moccu Machthéni. The Irish version dropped a line so that *canfaid míchrábud* of the present text is based upon *incantabit nefas* of Muirchú. The more archaic *tí* has been substituted for *bratt* of the Irish text. This emendation has been suggested by the alliterative principle upon which the poem is based and by the fact that the eighth century poet Blathmac son of Cú Brettan uses *tí chorcrae* of the purple cloak of the Passion. For *a méis*, 'from a table', of the present text, the Irish text has *a mias*, 'his table'. Muirchú has *a sua mensa*. The present edition is the first effort at reconstructing the original poem, which may well be sixth rather than seventh century. The poem is put in the mouth of a druidic opponent of St. Patrick, and is, of course, a satirical picture of a bishop saying Mass. It is important to remember that when this poem was written memories of paganism were by no means dead, and there was probably some hankering after the old ways. Note that I have translated *Amén, Amén,* as 'Be it thus. Be it thus'. Muirchú translated *'fiat, fiat'*. It seems to me that there is a pun in the original text: the congregation says

97

*Amén, Amén,* but the pagan listener hears the Irish words *Amin, Amin* 'Thus, thus' (?)

II-III. Probably c.600 See *The Problem of St. Patrick* (Carney), pp.131-3.

IV. Text from *Sancti Columbani Opera* (Walker), p.190.

V. From Glosses on Augustine (Carlsruhe), *Thesaurus Paleohibernicus* (Stokes and Strachan), II, p.7. The editors failed to notice the metrical character of the piece. Poem XIII is a longer poem in the same metre.

VI. See EIL, p.160. Dated by Murphy to the ninth or tenth century, but it is possibly earlier.

VII. Extracts from *The Poems of Blathmac son of Cú Brettan* (Carney), Irish Texts Society, Vol. XLVII. See also *Old Ireland and Her Poetry* (Carney) in *Old Ireland*, ed. Robert McNally S.J. (1965). Blathmac lived in the middle of the eighth century.

VIII. An extract from *Caoineadh na Maighdine*, a dramatic folk-prayer, still current. The present verses are as recorded by An Seabhac from the recital of Seán Bán O Conchobhair in 1902 (*An Seanchaidhe Muimhneach*, 1932, p.401).

IX, X. From the St. Gall Priscian, *Thesaurus Paleohibernicus* (Stokes and Strachan) II, p.290. For IX see EIL, p.4. Ninth century.

XI. See Kuno Meyer, *Four Old Irish Songs of Summer and Winter* (1903) p.18. Probably ninth century.

XII. Attributed to the wife of Aed mac Ainmirech who was slain in 598. Probably eighth century. Meyer, *Bruchstücke*, 89.

XIII. See Murphy EIL, p.82. In § 5 I have read *fírinne* for *fírithir*, assuming a mistranscription owing to *Cuirithir* in the preceding line.

XIV. Ninth or tenth century. Meyer, *Bruchstücke*, 160, Murphy EIM, p.59.

XV. Ninth century. See Murphy EIL, p.74. Here the quatrains corresponding to 27 and 35 of Murphy's text have been omitted. The text as given here differs in a number of important particulars from that of Murphy.

XVI.   Ninth or tenth century. See Meyer, *Bruchstücke*, 149, Murphy EIM, p.73.

XVII.   This poem, hitherto unpublished, is taken from National Library of Ireland Gaelic MS. I. The first quatrain is also found in Laud 610, the second in King's Inn MS. no. 12. In § 1 the MS. reads *in fót*, in § 4 *nochan fhuil*. The date would be about the eleventh or twelfth century, probably the former.

XVIII.   See *Eigse* II, pp.107-13.

XIX-XXIV.   About 845 Sedulius Scottus, with two companions, arrived on the continent, and was hospitably received by Hartgar, bishop of Liège, who made him *scholasticus* of the cathedral school, where he continued for about thirteen years. The text of the poems is as edited by Traube in *Poet. Lat. Car.* III. For an account of his life see the present writer's essay in *Old Ireland*, ed. Robert McNally S.J.

XXV.   Late tenth century. From Airbertach mac Coisse's lengthy geographical poem *Ro fessa hi curp domuin dúir*, Bodleian MS., Rawl. B 502, 77b.

XXVI,   See Murphy EIL, p.26. For the idea behind the poem see comment by the present writer in *Old Ireland*, ed. Robert McNally S.J., p.166.

XXVII.   See Murphy, EIL, p.10.

XXVIII.   See Murphy, EIL, p.50.

XXIX.   See my article *Eigse* IV, p.280. In the present text I have rejected a common emendation in § 2 of *a bé niata* to *a ben diatá*. The manuscript reading makes profound sense. The poet regards Crínóc as a warrior woman who undertakes the instruction of the young, as Scáthach did with Cú Chulainn.

XXX.   See *Eigse* I, p.248.

XXXI.   Eleventh century. From the Maynooth MS. 4a 10 10.

XXXII.   Ninth century. From the Codex Boernerianus, *Thesaurus Paleohibernicus* (Stokes and Strachan), II,p.296.

XXXIII.   See Mulchrone, *Caithréim Cellaig* (1933), p.13.

XXXIV.   Eleventh century (?). Meyer, *Bruchstücke*, 151.

XXXV.   Eleventh century. See Murphy, EIL, p.66.

XXXVI.   Eleventh century. See Murphy, EIL, p.64.

XXXVII.   c.1357. See E. Knott, *Irish Syllabic Poetry*, p.54.

XXXVIII.   Eighth century. See *Táin Bó Fraích* (M. Dillon), p.7.

XXXIX.   In 1381 Richard, bishop of Cloyne, celebrated a Mass in Dublin for the soul of Phillipa, the late Countess of March. He was charged that he 'did after beginning the accustomed preface introduce these words: *Eterne Deus* etc. and then omitted the divine words following but with a high voice said and sang these damnable words viz. *duo sunt, etc.*' The bishop was proceeded against for slander, schism and heresy and deprived of his see. See Edmund Curtis, *Calendar of Ormond Deeds*, II, p.168.

XL.   Folksong. See *Amhráin Mhuighe Seóla* (Mrs. Costelloe), p.72.

XLI.   Seventeenth century. See *Dánfhocail* (T. F O'Rahilly), p.31.

# Acknowledgements

Some of the translations presented here have appeared in other sources: *Ireland Harbinger of the Middle Ages*, Ludwig Bieler, Oxford University Press; *Old Ireland*, ed. Robert McNally S.J., M. H. Gill and Son Ltd., *Studies in Irish Literature and History*, James Carney, Dublin Institute for Advanced Studies; *The Dubliner*, winter 1964 (now *The Dublin Magazine*). For criticism and advice I am indebted to the Rev. Terence McCaughey. My wife also helped with criticism and proof reading.

JAMES CARNEY<br>
Dublin Institute for Advanced Studies.<br>
University of California, Los Angeles.